BULLMASTIFFS
KW-163

Title Page: *The head of the Bullmastiff is one of the breed's most dramatic features; the standards describe the skull as large and broad.*

Photography: *Isabelle Francais, William P. Gilbert, Vince Serbin, Sally Anne Thompson, and Louise van der Meid.*

Drawings: *Scott Boldt, Richard Crammer, Richard Davis, Andrew Prendimano, John Quinn, and Alexandra Suchenka.*

Distributed in the UNITED STATES by T.F.H. Publications, Inc., One T.F.H. Plaza, Neptune City, NJ 07753; in CANADA to the Pet Trade by H & L Pet Supplies Inc., 27 Kingston Crescent, Kitchener, Ontario N2B 2T6; Rolf C. Hagen Ltd., 3225 Sartelon Street, Montreal 382 Quebec; in CANADA to the Book Trade by Macmillan of Canada (A Division of Canada Publishing Corporation), 164 Commander Boulevard, Agincourt, Ontario M1S 3C7; in ENGLAND by T.F.H. Publications Limited, Cliveden House/Priors Way/Bray, Maidenhead, Berkshire SL6 2HP, England; in AUSTRALIA AND THE SOUTH PACIFIC by T.F.H. (Australia) Pty. Ltd., Box 149, Brookvale 2100 N.S.W., Australia; in NEW ZEALAND by Ross Haines & Son, Ltd., 18 Monmouth Street, Grey Lynn, Auckland 2, New Zealand; in the PHILIPPINES by Bio-Research, 5 Lippay Street, San Lorenzo Village, Makati Rizal; in SOUTH AFRICA by Multipet Pty. Ltd., 30 Turners Avenue, Durban 4001. Published by T.F.H. Publications, Inc. Manufactured in the United States of America by T.F.H. Publications, Inc.

BULLMASTIFFS

MARY A. PRESCOTT

A fair amount of wrinkles adorns the head, but a lack of foreface (like the Bulldog) is very undesirable. This handsome specimen is Ch. Brookhaven's Mean Mr. Mustard, owned by Paul Lipson.

Contents

Introducing the Bullmastiff

The Bullmastiff is one of the largest of all purebred dogs, and his heritage clearly shows his "bully" countenance. He is a noble, commanding animal and certainly one of the largest one might adopt as a satisfying companion. He is sedate in his role as caretaker and alert in his time-honored function as guardian and protector. His impressive size and regal bearing belie the swift motion of which he is capable when the spirit moves him. The docility attributed to him will be the prevailing attitude with which he greets each day, but it will quickly disappear from view if the well being of his loved ones is seriously threatened.

He is one of the most affectionate and responsive canines known to man. In his deep desire for human companionship, he will cheerfully tolerate an incredible amount of abuse from tots and toddlers. He is intelligent enough, however, to recognize that similar behavior need not be accepted from

Few puppies are as irresistible as Bullmastiff puppies—the dark muzzle, one the hallmarks of the breed, is prominent even on these two eight-week-old urchins. Owners, Thomas and Jean Widick.

This is Taghkanic's Bruno's Maximus, a 25-inch, 125-pound Bullmastiff, owned by Albert J. Batchelor. He took Reserve Winner's at Westminster.

adults; adults should dispense kindness, firmness, and the necessary discipline that must be a part of the daily lives of all large dogs. The happiest dogs are the ones who learn very early in their lives that there are rules and regulations which must be respected in order to earn acceptance as respectable citizens and neighbors in any household or community.

SPECIAL ABILITIES

The Bullmastiff's physical appearance is often the initial cause for attention from those in search of a pet, but his enormous size and tremendous physical strength are, quite often, enough to "put off" anyone who is unfamiliar with the great-hearted temperament behind this facade. Those who do gain the courage to adopt the dog into their daily lives more often than not become lifelong converts, and most who espouse ownership of this lesser known breed own or will own several, simultaneously or in succession. The winning combination of eye appeal, courage, and intelligence is quite enough to demonstrate the wisdom of selecting a

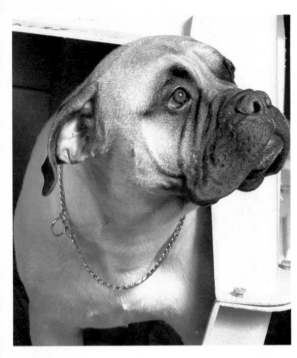

Ch. DJ's Show Some Respect getting ready to be transported to another show. Transportation carry cases such as this one are safe and efficient—they are available at pet shops and pet supply shops everywhere. Owner, Joann Duarte.

Bullmastiff as a family pet.

That same intelligence is the ingredient in the dog's character that makes for success in any formal training the owner may undertake. On the occasions when Bullmastiffs have been entered in obedience classes, graduation day usually sees them finishing high on the score list. More than one life has been saved by the Bullmastiffs' ability to track, and though they were neither bred to be nor are they known as hunters, they can be trained very successfully to small game.

PERSONALITY TRAITS

The Bullmastiff is a working dog and is happiest when he is given a job to do. Though he may take his orders from one master, he is not the sort one refers to as a ''one-man'' dog. He will live his life happily accepting attentions from all human beings, but will have a decided preference for his own family. He will live quite contentedly in a household where several other   pets are in residence; kittens may curl between his paws and parakeets may take biscuits from his dish. His daily companions become his very best friends.

In short, he knows in a very brief time who belongs to him. All his life, he will carry out the self-assigned task of safeguarding his family. The guarding instinct he will exhibit, often before he is out of puppyhood, may be carefully cultivated by those who are knowledgeable with regard to its use. The home will then be possessed of a caretaker unsurpassed in the world of canines.

HISTORY OF THE BREED

The Bullmastiff is British in origin, and is proudly claimed by his originators as "British to the core." He is a man-made breed, called into being by a definite need in an economic era of large game preserves and immense land holdings

Although the Bullmastiff may be as gentle as a pussycat, he has a will and the strength to impose it when desired. Owner, Joann Duarte.

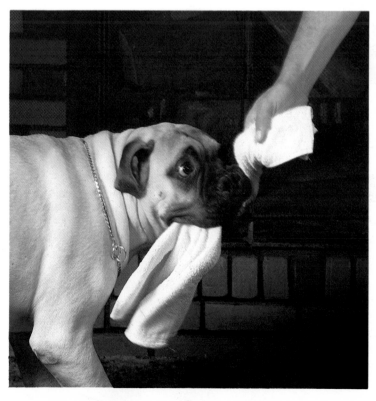

Introducing the Bullmastiff

which were robbed and plundered by poachers to an enormous degree. This was at least as far back as the mid-nineteenth century, and very probably extends many more years back beyond that point. The progenitors of the breed were carefully selected by those who studied the requirements for a dog who would serve as a deterrent to the gamekeeper's aggressive foe.

That their goal was quickly reached is a matter of record; the early breeders of the Bullmastiff designed him as a working dog. Though today's economic pattern has lessened the need for a dog to guard large estates, the Bullmastiff has suffered no loss of popularity. His main function in life today lies chiefly as pet and companion dog, although contemporary breeders have carefully continued a program designed to maintain the breed on a level of working capability. The results of the first fifty years or so of Bullmastiff history have

Through the years, the Bullmastiff has performed well in his given functions. Originally, he excelled as a working dog; today, more commonly, he is a companion and guardian and excels at these like no other.

The Bullmastiff's amenable disposition makes him a fine companion for children—he truly makes a reliable and good natured friend and protector of young ones.

been tremendously rewarding. The dog is held in high regard today, internationally, as a guard dog without peer.

The first step in producing the Bullmastiff was the carefully selected crossbreeding. The Bulldog was chosen for his speed, tenacity, and ferocity; the Mastiff for his great size, weight and power. The desired result was specified to be a dog who could catch, down, and hold a man without mauling.

In the early years, and lacking an official breed name, the Bullmastiff was referred to as a "holding dog" or "the gamekeeper's night dog." He was an animal of great courage and ferocity. The preferred brindled pigmentation most often exhibited by the early specimens served to foster the least possible attention to the dog. The color came from Bulldog genes, which also provided the type of mouth necessary to enable the dog to hold his quarry indefinitely while permitting respiratory function. Today's fanciers have long since discouraged the original hyphenated name Bull-Mastiff which signified the hybrid.

The shrewd old gamekeepers who adopted these dogs for protection knew what they wanted. They encouraged the necessary ferocity. Poaching on private property was an offense punishable by death in those days, and the thief who attempted such theft had nothing to lose in the attempt to gain his freedom, once discovered in the wrong. The arrival of this new breed soon sharply limited the number of those with the courage to venture against such dogs, and the saving of property and gamekeepers' lives became a matter of record.

Early breeders who realized what was at stake conscientiously applied themselves to constructive progress with each succeeding generation. After the necessary and successful early foundation established the Bullmastiff as approximately 40% Bulldog and 60% Mastiff, great care was taken in adhering to the clearly delineated path of perfection in breed type. There were others, less knowledgeable of breeding principles, who introduced, in haphazard fashion, the Great Dane, St. Bernard, Newfoundland, and the Bloodhound, which offered something of a setback for the beginning breed and must be accountable for today's occasional outcropping long coats and other imperfections which have no place in the breed picture.

The aggressive temperament of the dog was so successfully ingrained in early years as to give rise to the occasional "sharp" animal, even today. It is perhaps little understood that an efficient guard dog cannot be expected to evidence the true docility fondly favored by those understanding little of the breed foundation. The stable and dependable dog has always been held in highest regard by all sincerely desirous of promoting only the soundest of animals but who realize, however, that the complete elimination of "sparky" nature would quickly render the dog useless in performance.

POPULARITY IN ENGLAND AND THE UNITED STATES

Though there are diverse opinions on exactly when and where the breed was started, it is a matter of official record that the Bullmastiff was registered as a new breed in England, in 1924, after approximately a decade of breeding to fix type. The formal registration of sixty-three

Crates like this one holding DJ's Show Some Respect are useful in travelling and the like. Owner, J. Duarte.

Bullmastiffs by the English Kennel Club in 1925 attested to the fact of purebreeding for the required three generations, this being their requirement for proving the purebred status.

The greatest number of Bullmastiffs ever registered in England in modern times occurred in 1949, subsequent to the sharp reduction in numbers occasioned by several countries' utilizing them during the Second World War. Their growth in numbers, contrasted with that of other breeds, is rather limited. This is a distinct improvement, however, over the early years of the breed in the United States, where the registration of 25 or so in years subsequent to official American recognition in 1933 was cause for great rejoicing. The steady climb in popularity, however, is unmistakable.

As the breed became known in England as an efficient working dog, competition at dog shows became the natural testing place to establish quality in type. The first specimen to reach championship status in the history of the breed was a silver-fawn brindled English bitch, Ch. Farcroft Silvo, in 1928. Other countries adopting

The Bullmastiff is hailed as a purely British creation. The breed certainly has maintained a charming and gentlemanly disposition, traits unmistakably British.

Choosing your Bullmastiff puppy from a lot as adorable as this one would certainly be no easy task! Owner, Tom Widick.

the breed were, of course, somewhat slower to register their first champion specimens, with American breeders having to wait until 1949 to see their first Bullmastiff titled. This was male Ch. Lancelot of Northcastle, a 170-pound Mastiff-type dog, who would certainly not be acclaimed today.

BULLMASTIFFS IN THE WORLD

Bullmastiffs were first imported into the United States by Mr. John D. Rockefeller as guards for his huge country estate in Tarrytown, New York. Other areas to employ them were Africa, where they were used to guard the Kimberley diamond mines, a fact which served to display their usefulness and put them before the public eye. Their employment as guards during the Mau-Mau uprising in the 1950s further showed their distinct value as guards. Australia imported its first dogs prior to the Second World War, but these were not encouraged to reproduce, and it remained for later stock to lay the foundation for breeding in that country.

Introducing the Bullmastiff

A Mr. Russel of Melbourne, Australia, imported two dogs and two bitches of the world famous Blumas bloodline; Mr. and Mrs. Fortune of New South Wales brought in a bitch, Bulstaff Deliah of Buttonoak, bred by the renowned and respected Mr. and Mrs. Ralph Short of Bulstaff Kennels in Surrey England.

The Bullmastiff may now be found in Sri Lanka, India, Cambodia, France, Germany, Italy, Denmark, Canada, Mexico, and several of the South American countries. Today the dog is primarily a pet and companion dog who owes his popularity to a proud bearing, pleasing ways, and an excellent reputation.

Ch. DJ's Show Some Respect sharing the lens with Ch. Brookhaven's Huggy Cynthia, CD, owned by J. Duarte.

THE MODERN BULLMASTIFF

The modern Bullmastiff offers a color spectrum at wide variance from the early years, when the brindled pigmentation was most desired. The buying public's preference for the shades of fawn, which can range from a light grayish brown to a mahogany-red hue, and the reduced employment of dogs as night-roaming guards, have resulted in a decline in the number of dogs of deeper pigmentation. While there never has been a color program in the breed similar to that of Great Danes, the distinct value of retaining brindled Bullmastiffs is realized by many.

The modern dog show serves as a window through which the breed, still referred to as among the rare ones, can be viewed by the dog-loving public. Contemporary life not infrequently creates the type of family living where the breadwinner may be called away from home. Therefore, a strata of society is once again in need of the guard dog who continues to function in the specialty for which he was bred.

The most popular color for Bullmastiffs is fawn; however, many fanciers and breeders alike share an affinity for brindle.

Standard for the Breed

The Bullmastiff, like all other purebred dogs, is measured against a breed standard of perfection, a written description of what the ideal specimen should look like. Each dog-registering organization draws up a standard for each of the breeds of dog that it recognizes; however, these standards may vary, in the way they are worded, from registry to registry and from country to country. The breed has gained fanciers and admirers on both sides of the Atlantic and around the world. Likewise, the main registering bodies of the United States and Great Britain, the American Kennel Club and the Kennel Club, respectively, have accepted standards for the Bullmastiff. The British standard varies slightly from the American one in the following respects: *Eyes:* Set apart the width of muzzle with furrow between. *Ears:* Point level with eyes when alert. V-shaped or folded back small. *Faults:* Light or yellow eyes. Rose ears.

Standards have a tendency to change from time to time, as the various parent clubs perceive that a new wording or a new emphasis on a

The Bullmastiff was developed to be small enough to be agile and flexible, yet large enough to handle any prowler.

particular component will promote the continuance of type and soundness in the breed. If you are truly serious about showing your Bullmastiff, it is advised that you contact your local breed club for a copy of the most up-to-date standard. We present here both the AKC standard for the Bullmastiff and the Kennel Club standard for the sake of comparison and as a source of interest and information. If you do not plan to exhibit your Bullmastiff, we are confident that you will still find the following standards to your reading pleasure.

AKC STANDARD FOR THE BULLMASTIFF

General Appearance—That of a symmetrical animal, showing great strength; powerfully built but active. The dog is fearless yet docile, has endurance and alertness. The foundation breeding was 60% Mastiff and 40% Bulldog.

Head—*Skull:* Large, with a fair amount of wrinkles when alert; broad, with cheeks well developed. Forehead flat.

Muzzle: Broad and deep; its length, in comparison with that of the entire head, approximately as 1 is to 3. Lack of foreface with nostrils set on top of muzzle is a reversion to the Bulldog and is very undesirable. ***Nose:*** Black with nostrils large and broad.

This is Ch. Favodemel Calif of Baghdad, owned by Victor Zeoli, Jr., and bred by Favodemel Kennels.

Flews not too pendulous, stop moderate, and the mouth (bite) preferably level or slightly undershot. Canine teeth large and set wide apart. A dark muzzle is preferable. *Eyes:* Dark and of medium size. *Ears:* V-shaped and carried close to the cheeks, set on wide and high, level with occiput and cheeks, giving a square appearance to the skull; darker in color than the body and medium in size.

Neck—Slightly arched, of moderate length, very muscular, and almost equal in circumference to the skull.

Body—Compact. Chest wide and deep, with ribs well sprung and well set down between the forelegs *Forequarters:* Shoulders muscular but not loaded, and slightly sloping. Forelegs straight, well boned and set well apart; elbows square. Pasterns straight, feet of medium size, with round toes well arched. Pads thick and tough, nails black. *Back:* Short, giving the impression of a well-balanced dog. *Loins:* Wide, muscular and slightly arched, with fair depth of flank. *Hindquarters:* Broad and muscular with well-developed second thigh denoting power, but not too cumbersome. Moderate angulation at hocks. Cowhocks and splay feet are bad faults. *Tail:* Set on high, strong at the root and tapering to the hocks. It may be straight or curved, but never carried hound fashion.

Coat—Short and dense, giving good weather protection.

Color—Red, fawn, or brindle. Except for a very small white spot on the chest, white marking is considered a fault.

Size—Dogs, 25 to 27 inches at the shoulder, and 110 to 130 pounds weight. Bitches, 24 to 26 inches at the shoulder, and 100 to 120 pounds weight. Other things being equal, the heavier dog is favored.

Approved February 6, 1960.

THE KENNEL CLUB STANDARD FOR THE BULLMASTIFF

General Appearance: Powerful build, symmetrical, showing great strength, but not cumbersome, sound and active.

Characteristics: Powerful, enduring, active and reliable.

Temperament: High spirited, alert and faithful.

Head and Skull: Skull large

A dark muzzle with a black nose and broad, large nostrils is preferable. The Bullmastiff's cheeks are well-developed and the head should bear a square appearance. Owner, J. Duarte.

and square, viewed from every angle, fair wrinkle when interested, but not when in repose. Circumference of skull may equal height of dog measured at top shoulder; broad and deep with well-fixed cheeks. Pronounced stop. Muzzle short; distance from tip of nose to stop approximately one third of length from tip of nose to centre of occiput, broad under eyes and sustaining nearly same width to end of nose; blunt and cut off square, forming right angle with upper line of face, and at same time proportionate with skull. Underjaw broad to end. Nose broad with widely spreading nostrils; flat, neither pointed nor turned up in profile. Flews not pendulous, never hanging below level of lower jaw.

Eyes: Dark or hazel, of medium size, set apart the width of muzzle with furrow between. Light or yellow eyes highly undesirable.

Ears: V-shaped, folded back, set on wide and high, level of occiput giving square appearance to skull which is most important. Small and deeper in colour than body. Point of ear level with eye when alert. Rose ears highly undesirable.

Mouth: Level desired but slightly undershot allowed but not preferred. Canine teeth large and set wide apart, other teeth strong, even and well placed.

Neck: Well arched, moderate length, very muscular and almost equal to skull in circumference.

Forequarters: Chest, wide and deep, well let down between forelegs, with deep brisket. Shoulder muscular, sloping and powerful, not overloaded. Forelegs powerful and straight, well boned, set wide apart, presenting a straight front. Pasterns straight and strong.

Body: Back short and straight, giving compact carriage, but not so short as to interfere with activity. Roach and sway backs highly undesirable.

Hindquarters: Loins wide and muscular with fair depth of flank. Hindlegs strong and muscular, with well-developed second thighs, denoting power and activity, not cumbersome. Hocks moderately bent. Cowhocks highly undesirable.

Feet: Well arched, cat-like, with rounded toes, pads hard. Dark toenails desirable.

Splayed feet highly undesirable.

Tail: Set high, strong at root and tapering, reaching to hocks, carried straight or curved, but not hound fashion. Crank tails highly undesirable.

Gait/Movement: Movement indicates power and sense of purpose. When moving straight neither front nor hindlegs should cross or plait, right front and left rear leg rising and falling at same time. A firm backline unimpaired by powerful thrust from hindlegs denoting a balanced and harmonious movement.

Coat: Short and hard, weather resistant, lying flat to body. Long, silky or woolly coats highly undesirable.

Colour: Any shade of brindle, fawn or red; colour to be pure and clear. A slight white marking on chest permissible. Other white markings undesirable. Black muzzle essential, toning off towards eyes, with dark markings around eyes contributing to expression.

Size: Height at shoulder: Dogs 63.5-68.5 cm (25-27 inches); bitches 61-66 cm (24-26 inches). Weight: Dogs 49.9-59 kg (110-130 lbs); bitches 41-49.9 kg (90-110 lbs).

Faults: Any departure from the foregoing points should be considered a fault and the seriousness with which the fault should be regarded should be in exact proportion to its degree.

Note: Male animals should have two apparently normal testicles fully descended into the scrotum.

The Bullmastiff's gait indicates power and a sense of purpose—two qualities these two seem to have cornered the market on.

Bullmastiff as a Breed

TEMPERAMENT

The temperament of the Bullmastiff is perhaps the most appealing part of the total picture he presents. He is a steady, stable animal, completely lacking in excitability. His intelligence, plus his readiness to use it, is certainly "selling" him as the ideal pet. He adores children and will tolerate an incredible amount of abuse from them. He is completely dependable, but the unfortunate midnight prowler has much to worry about. A Bullmastiff will seldom bark, and never will he do so without reason. When he does give voice, it is a good idea to investigate the cause. The bark is unique in that a different one is given for various causes, but one had best give heed to the deeply resonant full voice which alerts the family to invasion by a caller.

The docility which is mentioned in the American standard for the breed can be misleading. It does not appear in the English standard, which depicts the Bullmastiff as "high spirited, reliable, active, enduring, alert." True docility would be unbecoming in our dog.

Some understanding of the foundation of this fine breed will aid the new owner in sensible realization of the temperament he may expect. The cross of Bulldog and Mastiff produced dogs that were holy terrors. Subsequent generations produced by knowledgeable breeders weeded out much of this tendency, though one still notices little tolerance for strange dogs, particularly on the part of mature dogs and bitches. However, the fact remains that a Bullmastiff may be raised satisfactorily with several other pets. Any dog that has made its name as a guard dog cannot be expected to take to strange canines on sight.

Having gained some understanding of the breed and how it differs from other types of dogs, one is urged to accept the idea that all large canines are molded into much more acceptable and delightful companions if properly educated to their role in life.

Facing page: *One of the breeds hailed by many as a "gentle giant," the Bullmastiff possesses a high-spirited temperament yet is rather docile in its fearlessness.*

Puppies at eight weeks of age will need to be fed four times a day—they are nearly weaned from their mothers by three months.

The basic obedience commands will be readily accepted by a six-month-old puppy. This same puppy will often be seventy pounds in weight. Therefore, it is important that the novice Bullmastiff owner establish his right to rule from the earliest days of puppyhood.

Obedience training is recommended for all dogs, and particularly for large breeds. One may not depend on physical strength to compel good behavior with a dog any more than with one's rambunctious strapping teenager. A well-bred dog which has been schooled to a realization to his full potential as a companion to his family is a joy and a delight to all who live with him.

GROOMING

Daily grooming requires a minimum effort with a Bullmastiff, whose short dense coat is probably one of the easiest to care for. A ten-minute daily brushing with a hound glove will keep him sleek and glossy. The occasional use of a stripping comb, similar to that used for terrier coats, will remove dead hair and encourage the new growth, which occurs usually in the spring, when either a gradual or definite "molting" may be noticed. Soap and water baths are not advised, generally speaking, as they remove all the natural oils in the skin and hair. It is better to clean the dog with one of several good preparations from your local pet shop. A dry, rough coat at any time signals the possibility of intestinal parasites, although it may simply indicate that the diet needs improvement.

One incontestable asset of the Bullmastiff is his easy-care coat. Regular brushing should eliminate the need for frequent bathing.

SKIN ATTENTION

During the warm weather, make an effort to detect the presence of fleas or ticks in your dog's coat. The tick is gradually increasing in population wherever one looks, and he is a carrier of dreaded disease. He will bury his head in the skin and withdraw blood. If his presence goes undiscovered for any length of time, he will constitute a real threat to any dog's health. Run your fingers through the dog's coat, and view with suspicion any small lump—it may be a tick. This

As a general rule, bathing is not recommended. Soap tends to dry the natural oils in a dog's coat; not to mention, the practical consideration of bathing a dog this size. Other options such as dry baths are available at pet stores.

insect can be removed in several ways, but perhaps the best method is to spray the dog weekly with one of the products offered for this purpose.

Many of the summer skin problems which afflict the densely coated breeds, called by many names such as "hot

28

The Bullmastiff is a "manufactured" breed created to serve man—a capacity in which it surpasses all other breeds.

spots," "summer eczema," "moist eczema," are caused by nothing more complicated than infestation by fleas. Even though great care in cleanliness may be exercised, fleas may be picked up in grass, from other dogs when at play, and from the new hatchings of adult fleas previously destroyed. Again, the dog must be treated regularly with a specific product for this parasite—and his bed, his toys, and his

Your Bullmastiff should be taught the rules of the house while he is still a puppy—a full-grown Bullmastiff may be difficult to convince to leaving the comfort of your favorite chair.

sleeping quarters, too. One must gain some understanding of the life cycle of the flea in order to eliminate the problem, but the measures employed will add up to a healthier and happier pet.One very appealing item in the care of the Bullmastiff is that there is no trimming, clipping, or cropping of ears. The tail also remains undocked.

A STEP-BY-STEP GROOMING PROCEDURE

The following tools and equipment will be needed in the grooming of your Bullmastiff:
- *Sisal (natural bristle) brush*
- *Medicated ear powder*
- *Nail clipper*
- *Medicated talcum powder*
- *Eye drops (eye stain remover)*
- *Scissors*
- *Lanolin coat conditioner*
- *Chamois cloth*
- *Cotton balls*

1. Thoroughly brush the entire coat.

2. Clean the ears using the medicated ear powder.

3. Clean the eyes by wiping with eye stain remover on cotton. This will also help to remove any stains from the

Regularly trimming your Bullmastiff's nails is necessary.

corners of the eyes.

4. Cut the tips of the toenails with the nail clipper, being careful not to cut the quick.

5. Using a damp cotton ball, clean the insides of the lips, making certain that you remove any trapped food particles.

6. With the scissors clip the whiskers from the muzzle, under the chin, and from the sides of the face and above the eyes.

7. Put a cotton ball in each ear (this prevents water from entering the ear canal) and bathe the dog. Cage dry him.

8. Clean the furrows on the face with cotton that has been moistened with eye stain remover; daily use of this product, or medicated talcum powder, on the furrows will keep them clean and help prevent soreness and infection.

9. Put a few drops of a lanolin coat conditioner into the palms of your hands, rub together lightly, and gently massage into the coat.

10. Brush the coat with a sisal brush (to distribute the conditioner) and then rub the coat with the chamois cloth to give it a nice sheen.

Ch. Brookhaven's Mean Mr. Mustard is a fine example of a brindle Bullmastiff. The breed's eyes should not be light but rather should be dark or hazel. Mr. Mustard's pensive brown eyes blend in beautifully with his coat. Owner, Paul Lipson.

Selecting Your Dog

Now that you have decided which dog breed suits your needs, your lifestyle, and your own temperament, there will be much to consider before you make your final purchase. Buying a puppy on impulse may only cause heartbreak later on; it makes better sense to put some real thought into your canine investment, especially since it is likely that he will share many happy years with you. Which individual will you choose as your adoring companion? Ask yourself some questions as you analyze your needs and preferences for a dog, read all that you can about your particular breed, and visit as many dog shows as possible. At the shows you will be surrounded by people who can give you all the details about the breed you are interested in buying. Decide if you want a household pet, a dog for breeding, or a show dog. Would you prefer a male or female? Puppy or adult?

If you buy from a breeder, ask him to help you with your decision. When you have settled on the dog you want, discuss with him the dog's temperament, the animal's positive and negative aspects, any health problems it might have, its feeding and grooming requirements, and whether the dog has been immunized. Reputable breeders will be willing to answer any questions you might have that pertain to the dog you have selected, and often they will make themselves available if you call for advice or if you encounter problems after you've made your purchase.

If you have chosen a Bullmastiff as the breed of dog for you, you have gained a competent and reliable guardian and companion.

A bit too big?
A little **too** small.
Too fuzzy for me!
Too fat to crawl.

Before you wrap it tight
And crate it home,
Behold its appetite
And room to roam.

A sloppy yap, a barking slur,
Puppy eyes to be let free,
A him? a her? an unmarked cur,
Let's pout to see its pedigree.

The perfect pet quest:
Which pup for me is best?

ANDREW DE PRISCO

Selecting Your Dog

Most breeders want to see their dogs placed in loving, responsible homes; they are careful about who buys their animals. So as the dog's new owner, prepare yourself for some interrogation from the breeder.

WHERE TO BUY

You can choose among several places to buy your dog. Many people think of their local pet shop as the first source for buying a puppy, and very often they're

The Bullmastiff takes great pride in protecting his owner and his owner's property. Many Bullmastiff owners claim their breed is the most competent of all canine guards. Owner, Vic Zeoli.

right; you should remember, however, that a pet shop cannot possibly stock all breeds of dog. If your pet shop does not carry the type of dog you desire, there are other places to look. One is a kennel whose business is breeding show-quality dogs; such kennels may have extra pups for sale. Another source is the one-dog owner who wants to sell the puppies from an occasional litter to pay the expenses of his small-scale breeding operation. To find such kennels and part-time breeders and hobbyists, check the classified section of your local newspaper or look in your telephone directory.

Whichever source you choose, you can usually tell in a very short time whether the puppies will make healthy and happy pets. If they are clean, plump, and lively, they are probably in good health. At the breeder's you will have the advantage of seeing the puppies' dam and perhaps their sire and other relatives. Remember that the mother, having just raised a demanding family, may not be looking her best; but if she is sturdy, friendly, and well-mannered, her puppies should be too. If you feel that something is lacking in the care or condition of the dogs, it is better to look elsewhere than to buy hastily and regret it afterward. Buy a healthy dog with a good disposition, one that has been

Whether your Bullmastiff is a pet- or show-quality dog, you can be sure he will make a loving and agreeable friend.

properly socialized and likes being around people.

If you cannot find the dog you want locally, write to the secretary of the national breed club or kennel club and ask for names of breeders near you or to whom you can write for information. Puppies are often shipped, sight unseen, from reputable breeders. In these instances, pictures and pedigree information are usually sent beforehand to help you decide.

Breeders can supply you with further details and helpful guidance, if you require it. Many breed clubs provide a puppy referral service, so you may want to look into this before making your final decision.

PET OR SHOW DOG

Conscientious breeders strive to maintain those desirable qualities in their breed. At the same time, they are always working to improve on what they have already achieved, and they do this by referring to the breed standard of perfection. The standard describes the ideal dog, and those animals that come close to the ideal are generally selected as show

Owners of purebred dogs too often forget that all breeds of dog are interrelated. The ancient canine that is the believed ancestor of all dogs is known as Tomarctus. As packs traveled and inhabited various lands, types evolved through the process of adaptation. Later, as dogs and man joined forces, type became further diversified. This chart sketches one commonly accepted theory of the domesticated dog's development. Where does your dog fit in? With a few exceptions, dogs evolve or change as a result of a specific functional need.

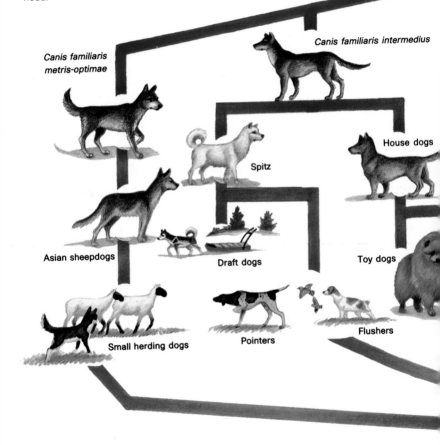

Canis familiaris intermedius

Canis familiaris metris-optimae

House dogs

Spitz

Asian sheepdogs

Draft dogs

Toy dogs

Small herding dogs

Pointers

Flushers

Tomarctus

Canis familiaris leineri

Canis familiaris inostranzewi

Russian Tracker

Molossian

Scenthounds

Sighthound
prototypes

Mastiffs

Sighthounds

Terriers

Bulldogs

Retrievers

Large herding dogs

stock; those that do not are culled and sold as pets. Keep in mind that pet-quality purebred dogs are in no way less healthy or attractive than show-quality specimens. It's just that the pet may have undesirable features (such as ears that are too large

Bullmastiffs can be overwhelmingly affectionate at times. This dog is elated that her master has finally come home to play with her.

or eyes that are the wrong color for its breed) which would be faults in the show ring. Often these so-called "flaws" are detectable only by experienced breeders or show judges. Naturally the more perfect animal, in terms of its breed standard, will cost more—even though he seems almost identical to his pet-quality littermate.

If you think you may eventually want to show your dog or raise a litter of puppies, by all means buy the best you can afford. You will save expense and disappointment later on. However, if the puppy is strictly to be a pet for the children, or a companion for you, you can afford to look for a bargain. The pup which is not show material, or the older pup for which there is often less demand, or the grown dog which is not being used for breeding are occasionally available and offer opportunities to save money. Remember that your initial investment may be a bargain, but it takes good food and care— and plenty of both—to raise a healthy, vigorous puppy through its adulthood.

Facing page: *The breed's alert and high-energy temperament makes them ideal for a variety of working capacities—of course, guard work has become one of the breed's specialties. Owners, Julio and Isabelle Esteban, Jr.*

The price you pay for your dog is little compared to the love and devotion he will return over the many years he'll be with you. With proper care and affection, your pup should live to a ripe old age; thanks to modern veterinary science and improvements in canine nutrition, dogs today are better maintained and live longer. It is not uncommon to see dogs living well into their teens.

Generally speaking, small dogs live longer than big ones. With love and the proper care any dog will live to its optimum age. Many persons, however,

opt for a particular breed because of its proven longevity. This, of course, is purely a personal decision.

MALE OR FEMALE

If you intend to breed your dog someday, by all means buy a female. You can find a suitable mate without difficulty when the time comes, and you'll have the pleasure of raising a litter of puppies. If you don't want to raise puppies, however, your female should be spayed so that she will remain a healthy, lively pet. Similarly, a male purchased as a pet, rather than as a stud

This illustration of the dog's skeleton and vital organs reveals the distinctive construction of the dog. Veterinary medicine, largely devoted to the better health of your dog, continues to make advances that promise even greater canine longevity.

According to some astrologers, dogs too are affected by their zodiac sign. If you follow the stars, be sure to select a dog born under a sky compatible with that of your birth date.

dog, should be castrated. The female is smaller than the male and generally quieter. She has less tendency to roam in search of romance, but a properly trained male can be a charming pet and has a certain difference in temperament that is appealing to many people. Male versus female is chiefly a matter of personal choice; both make fine companions.

ADULT OR PUP

Whether to buy a grown dog or a young puppy is another question. It is surely an undeniable pleasure to watch your dog grow from a lively pup to a mature, dignified dog. If you don't have the time to spend on the more frequent meals, housebreaking, and other training a puppy needs in order to become a dog you can be proud of, then choose an older, partly-trained adolescent or a grown dog. If you want a show dog, remember that no one, not even an expert, can predict with one hundred percent accuracy what a puppy will be like when he grows up. The dog may seem to exhibit show potential *most* of the time, but six months is the earliest age for the would-be exhibitor to select a prospect and know that its future is in the show ring.

If you have a small child, it is best to get a puppy big enough to defend itself, one not less than four or five months old.

Older children will enjoy playing with and helping to take care of a baby pup; but at less than four months, a puppy wants to do little else but eat and sleep, and he must be protected from teasing and overtiring. You cannot expect a very young child to understand that a puppy is a fragile living being; to the youngster he is a toy like his

Training should begin when your dog is still quite young. Fortunately for the Bullmastiff owner, the breed is both easily trainable and obedient.

Sporting an impressive physique and a handsome head, the Bullmastiff has delighted many newcomers to the breed.

stuffed dog. Children, therefore, must learn how to handle and care for their young pets.

We recommend you start with a puppy so that you can raise and train it according to the rules you have established in your own home. While a dog is young, its behavior can be more easily shaped by the owner, whereas an older dog , although trainable, may be a bit set in his ways.

WHAT TO LOOK FOR IN A PUPPY

In choosing a puppy, assuming that it comes from healthy, well-bred parents, look for one that is friendly and outgoing. The biggest pup in the litter is apt to be somewhat coarse as a grown dog, while the appealing "runt of the litter" may turn out to be a timid shadow—or have a Napoleonic complex! If you want a show dog and have no experience in choosing a prospect, study the breed standard and listen carefully to the breeder on the finer points of show conformation. A breeder's prices will be in accord with his puppies' expected worth, and he will be honest with you about each pup's potential because it is to his own advantage. He wants his top-quality show puppies placed in the public eye to reflect glory on him—and to attract future buyers. Why should he sell a potential show champion to someone who just wants a pet?

Now that you have paid your money and made your choice, you are ready to depart with puppy, papers, and instructions. Make sure that you know the youngster's feeding routine, and

take along some of his food. For the trip home, place him in a comfortable, sturdy carrier. Do not drive home with a puppy on your lap! If you'll be travelling for a few hours, at the very least bring along a bottle of water from the breeder and a small water dish.

PEDIGREE AND REGISTRATION

Owners of puppies are often misled by sellers with such ruses as leading the owner to believe his dog is something special. The term *pedigree papers* is quite different from the term *registration papers*. A pedigree is nothing more than a statement made by the breeder of the dog;

Dog shows are fascinating to both the participants and the spectators. If you have never attended a dog show, you are missing an important part of the canine world. This is the Crufts Show in England.

Pedigree papers can trace a dog's lineage back several generations. They do not, however, guarantee that a puppy is of good quality or sound health.

and it is written on special pedigree blanks, which are readily available from any pet shop or breed club, with the names of several generations from which the new puppy comes. It records your puppy's ancestry and other important data, such as the pup's date of birth, its breed, its sex, its sire and dam, its breeder's name and address, and so on. If your dog has had purebred champions in his background, then the pedigree papers are valuable as evidence of the good breeding behind your dog; but if the names on the pedigree paper are meaningless, then so is the paper itself. Just because a dog has a pedigree doesn't necessarily mean he is registered with a kennel club.

Registration papers from the American Kennel Club or the United Kennel Club in the United States or The Kennel Club of Great Britain attest to the fact that the mother and father of your puppy were purebred dogs of the breed represented by your puppy and that they were registered with a particular club. Normally every registered dog also has a complete pedigree available. Registration papers, which you receive when you buy a puppy, merely enable you to register your puppy. Usually the breeder has registered only the litter, so it is the new owner's responsibility to register and name an individual pup. The papers should be filled out and sent to the appropriate address printed on the application, along with the fee required for the registration. A certificate of registration will then be sent to you.

Pedigree and registration, by the way, have nothing to do with licensing, which is a local regulation applying to purebred and mongrel alike. Find out what the local ordinance is in your town or city and how it applies to your dog; then buy a license and keep it on your dog's collar for identification.

The clear, alert eyes of this brindle Bullmastiff reveal a state of watchful attentiveness. As lovable and playful as he is dependable and imposing, the Bullmastiff is truly an outstanding canine.

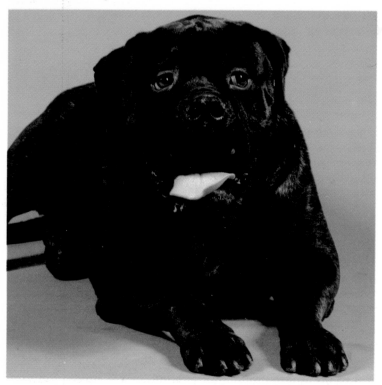

The New Family Member

Although no one can guarantee that your new Bullmastiff will grow to be as handsome as Ch. Favodemel Calif of Baghdad, you can be certain that he will be unique and wonderful in his own way.

At long last, the day you have all been waiting for, your new puppy will make its grand entrance into your home. Before you bring your companion to its new residence, however, you must plan carefully for its arrival. Keep in mind that the puppy will need time to adjust to life with a different owner. He may seem a bit apprehensive about the strange surroundings in which he finds himself, having spent the first few weeks of life with his dam and littermates, but in a couple of days, with love and patience on your part, the transition will be complete.

First impressions are important, especially from the puppy's point of view, and these may very well set the pattern of his future relationship with you. You must be consistent in the way you handle your pet so that he learns what is expected of him. He must come to trust and respect you as his keeper and master. Provide him with proper care and attention, and you will be rewarded with a loyal companion for many years. Considering the needs of your puppy and planning ahead will surely make the change from his former home to his new one easier.

ADVANCE PREPARATION

In preparing for your puppy's arrival, perhaps more important than anything else is to find out from the seller how the pup was maintained. What brand of food was offered and when and how often was the puppy fed? Has

A crate, for home and travel, is standard equipment and makes an excellent gift for the new dog owner.

the pup been housebroken; if so, what method was employed? Attempt to continue whatever routine was started by the person from whom you bought your puppy; then, gradually, you can make those changes that suit you and your lifestyle. If, for example, the puppy has been paper trained, plan to stock up on newspaper. Place this newspaper toilet facility in a selected spot so that your puppy learns to use the designated area as his "bathroom." And keep on hand a supply of the dog food to which he is accustomed, as a sudden switch to new food could cause digestive upsets.

Another consideration is sleeping and resting quarters. Be sure to supply a dog bed for your pup, and introduce him to his special cozy corner so that he

A warm bed, equipped with a ticking clock, chew bone, and safe dog toy, can help a pup feel secure and welcome in its new home.

knows where to retire when he feels like taking a snooze. You'll need to buy a collar (or harness) and leash, a safe chew item (such as Nylabone® or Gumabone®), and a few grooming tools as well. A couple of sturdy feeding dishes, one for food and one for water, will be needed; and it will be necessary, beforehand, to set up a feeding station.

FINDING A VETERINARIAN

An important part of your preparations should include finding a local veterinarian who can provide quality health care in the form of routine check-ups, inoculations, and prompt medical attention in case of illness or an emergency. Find out if the animal you have selected has been vaccinated against canine diseases, and make certain you secure all health certificates at the time of purchase. This information will be valuable to your veterinarian, who will want to know the puppy's complete medical history. Incidentally, don't wait until your puppy becomes sick before you seek the services of a vet; make an appointment for your pup before or soon after he takes up residence with you so that he starts out with a clean bill of health in his new home.

CHILDREN AND PUPPIES

Prepare the young members of the household on pet care. Children should learn not only to love their charges but to respect them and treat them with the consideration one would give all living things. It must be emphasized to youngsters that the puppy has certain needs, just as humans have, and all family members must take an active role in ensuring that these needs are met. Someone must feed the puppy. Someone must walk him a couple of times a day or clean up after him if he is trained to relieve himself on newspaper. Someone must groom his coat, clean his ears, and clip his nails from time to time. Someone

must see to it that the puppy gets sufficient exercise and attention each day.

A child who has a pet to care for learns responsibility; nonetheless, parental guidance is an essential part of his learning experience. Many a child has been known to "love a pet to death," squeezing and hugging the animal in ways which are irritating or even painful. Others have been found guilty of teasing, perhaps unintentionally, and disturbing their pet while the animal is eating or resting. One must teach a child, therefore, when and how to gently stroke and fondle a puppy. In time, the child can learn how to carefully pick up and handle the pup. A dog should always be supported with both hands, *not* lifted by the scruff of the neck. One hand placed under the chest, between the front legs, and the other hand supporting the dog's rear end will be comfortable and will restrain the animal as you hold and carry him. Always demonstrate to children the proper way to lift a dog.

BE A GOOD NEIGHBOR

For the sake of your dog's safety and well being, don't allow him to wander onto the property of others. Keep him confined at all times to your own yard or indoors where he won't become a nuisance. Consider what

The Bullmastiffs are happy-go-lucky canines who are sincerely responsive to human companionship. They may often be one-man dogs but surely make an attempt to accept all members of the household.

Many dangers lurk around the house. Keep all poisonous substances and sharp objects away from your curious pup.

dangers lie ahead for an unleashed dog that has total freedom of the great outdoors, particularly when he is unsupervised by his master. There are cars and trucks to dodge on the streets and highways. There are stray animals with which to wrangle. There are poisons all around, such as car antifreeze in driveways or toxic plants and shrubs, which, if swallowed, could prove fatal. There are dognappers and sadistic people who may steal or bring harm to your beloved pet. In short, there are all sorts of nasty things waiting to hurt him. Did you know that if your dog consumes rotting garbage, there is the possibility he could go into shock or even die? And are you aware that a dog left to roam in a wooded area or field could become infected with any number of parasites if he plays with or ingests some small prey, such as a rabbit, that might be carrying these parasitic organisms? A thorn from a rosebush imbedded in the dog's foot pad, tar from a newly paved road stuck to his coat, and a wound inflicted by a wild animal all can be avoided if you take the precaution of keeping your dog in a safe enclosure where he will be protected from such dangers. Don't let your dog run loose; he is likely to stray from home and get into all sorts of trouble.

Clockwise from upper right: *pokeweed, jimson weed, foxglove, and yew.* *If ingested, a toxic plant can be dangerous to your dog.*

The New Family Member

GETTING ACQUAINTED

Plan to bring your new pet home in the morning so that by nightfall he will have had some time to become acquainted with you and his new environment. Avoid introducing the pup to the family around holiday time, since all of the extra excitement will only add to the confusion and frighten him. Let the puppy enter your home on a day when the

Resist the temptation to handle him too much during these first few days. And, if there are other dogs or animals around the house, make certain all are properly introduced. If you observe fighting among the animals, or some other problem, you may have to separate all parties until they learn to accept one another. Remember that neglecting your other pets while

routine is normal. For those people who work during the week, a Saturday morning is an ideal time to bring the puppy to his new home; this way he has the entire weekend to make adjustments before being left alone for a few hours, come Monday morning.

Let the puppy explore, under your watchful eye of course, and let him come to know his new home without stress and fear.

The Bullmastiff exists today because early British breeders selectively crossed two prominent national breeds: the Bulldog, for its tenacity and speed, and the Mastiff, for its great size and power. The result, of course, was the wonderful Bullmastiff we know today.

Facing page: *The Bullmastiff's coat is short and dense and provides him with adequate protection from the elements.*

showering the new puppy with extra attention will only cause animosity and jealousy. Make an effort to pay special attention to the other animals as well.

On that eventful first night, try not to give in and let the puppy sleep with you; otherwise, this could become a difficult habit to break. Let him cry and whimper, even if it means a night of restlessness for the entire family. Some people have had success with putting a doll or a hot water bottle wrapped in a towel in the puppy's bed as a surrogate mother, while others have placed a ticking alarm clock in the bed to simulate the heartbeat of the pup's dam and littermates. Remember that this furry little fellow is used to the warmth and security of his mother and siblings, so the adjustment to sleeping alone will take time. Select a location away from drafts and away from the feeding station for placement of his dog bed. Keep in mind, also, that the bed should be roomy enough for him to stretch out in; as he grows older, you may need to supply a larger one.

Prior to the pup's arrival, set up his room and partition it the way you would to keep an infant out of a particular area. You may want to keep his bed, his feeding station, and his toilet area all in the same room—in separate locations—or you may want to set the feeding station up in your kitchen, where meals for all family members are served. Whatever you decide, do it ahead of time so you will have that much less to worry about when your puppy finally moves in with you.

Above all else, be patient with your puppy as he adjusts to life in his new home. If you purchase a pup that is not housebroken, you will have to spend time with the dog—just as you would with a small child—until he develops proper toilet habits. Even a housebroken puppy may feel nervous in strange new surroundings and have an occasional accident. Praise and encouragement will elicit far better results than punishment or scolding. Remember that your puppy wants nothing more than to please you, thus he is anxious to learn the behavior that is required of him.

Feeding Requirements

Perhaps more than any other single aspect of your dog's development, proper feeding requires an educated and responsible dog owner. The importance of nutrition on your dog's bone and muscle growth cannot be over emphasized.

Soon after your puppy comes to live with you, he will need to be fed. Remember to ask the seller what foods were given to the youngster and stay with that diet for a while. It is important for the puppy to keep eating and to avoid skipping a meal, so entice him with the food to which he is accustomed. If you prefer to switch to some other brand of dog food, each day begin to add small quantities of the new brand to the usual food offering. Make the portions of the new food progressively larger until the pup is weaned from his former diet.

What should you feed the puppy and how often? His diet is really quite simple and relatively inexpensive to prepare. Puppies need to be fed small portions at frequent intervals, since they are growing and their activity level is high. You must ensure that your pup gains weight steadily; with an adult dog, however, growth slows down and weight must be regulated to prevent obesity and a host of other problems. At one time, it was thought that home-cooked meals were the answer, with daily rations of meat,

The canine digestive system is adapted for omnivorous eating habits. Canines require both animal and vegetable matter for good health.

vegetables, egg yolk, cereal, cheese, brewer's yeast, and vitamin supplements. With all of the nutritionally complete commercial dog food products readily available, these time-consuming preparations really are unnecessary now. A great deal of money and research has resulted in foods that we can serve our dogs with confidence and pride; and most of these commercial foods have been developed along strict guidelines according to the size, weight, and age of your dog. These products are reasonably priced, easy to find, and convenient to store.

THE PUPPY'S MEALS

After a puppy has been fully weaned from its mother until approximately three months of age, it needs to be fed four times a day. In the morning and evening offer kibble (dog meal) soaked in hot water or broth, to which you have added some canned meat-based food or fresh raw meat cut into small chunks. At noon and bedtime feed him a bit of kibble or whole-grain cereal moistened with milk (moistening, by the way, makes the food easier to digest, since dogs don't typically chew their food). From three to six months, increase the portion size and

The steady, unexcitable temperament characteristic of the breed can already be seen in the tranquil face of this pup. Even at such an early age, a puppy will divulge particular breed traits.

The Bullmastiff's back is short and straight, giving compact carriage. An undeniable air of nobility accompanies the breed's composure.

offer just three meals—one milk and two meat. At six months, two meals are sufficient; at one year, a single meal can be given, supplemented with a few dry biscuits in the morning and evening. During the colder months, especially if your dog is active, you might want to mix in some wheat germ oil or corn oil or bacon drippings with the meal to add extra calories. Remember to keep a bowl of cool, fresh water on hand always to help your dog regulate its body temperature and to aid in digestion.

From one year on, you may continue feeding the mature dog a single meal (in the evening, perhaps, when you have your supper), or you may prefer to divide this meal in two, offering half in the morning and the other half at night. Keep in mind that while puppies require foods in small chunks, or nuggets, older dogs can handle larger pieces of food at mealtime. Discuss your dog's feeding schedule with your veterinarian; he can make suggestions about the right diet for your particular canine friend.

COMPARISON SHOPPING
With so many fine dog-food products on the market today, there is something for

Feeding Requirements

everyone's pet. You may want to serve dry food "as is" or mix it with warm water or broth. Perhaps you'll choose to combine dry food with fresh or canned preparations. Some canned foods contain all meat, but they are not complete; others are mixtures of meat and grains, which have been fortified with additional nutrients to make them more complete and balanced. There are also various packaged foods that can be served alone or as supplements and that can be left out for a few hours without spoiling. This self-feeding method, which works well for dogs that are not prone to weight problems, allows the animal to serve himself whenever he feels hungry. Many people who work during the day find these dry or semi-moist rations convenient to use, and these foods are great to bring along if you travel with your dog.

Be sure to read the labels carefully before you make your dog-food purchases. Most

Pet shops offer a large selection of quality bowls that are efficient and affordable. Offered in a wide variety of colors, bowls are easy to coordinate.

Vegetables, grains, meats and dairy products are all vital components of your dog's diet. Fortunately, commercial dog foods are nutritionally balanced and easily digestible.

reputable pet-food manufacturers list the ingredients and the nutritional content right on the can or package. Instructions are usually included so that you will know how much to feed your dog to keep him thriving and in top condition. A varied, well-balanced diet that supplies the proper amounts of protein, carbohydrate, fat, vitamins, minerals, and water is important to keep your puppy healthy and to guarantee his normal development. Adjustments to the diet can be made, under your veterinarian's supervision, according to the individual puppy, his rate of growth, his activity level, and so on. Liquid or powder vitamin and mineral supplements, or those in tablet form, are available and can be given if you need to feel certain that the diet is balanced.

For the love, protection, and companionship that your Bullmastiff provides, properly caring for him is but a small price to pay. Owner, Joann Duarte.

DEVELOPING GOOD EATING HABITS

Try to serve your puppy his meals at the same time each day and in the same location so that he will get used to his daily routine and develop good eating habits. A bit of raw egg, cottage cheese, or table scraps (leftover food from your own meals) can

Feeding your dog need not be a messy chore, provided that non-tipping, easy-clean bowls are used for each meal.

be offered from time to time; but never accustom your dog to eating human "junk food." Cake, candy, chocolate, soda, and other snack foods are for people, not dogs. Besides, these foods provide only "empty" calories that your pet doesn't need if he is to stay healthy. Avoid offering spicy, fried, fatty, or starchy foods; rather, offer leftover meats, vegetables, and gravies. Get in the habit of feeding your puppy or your grown dog his *own* daily meals of dog food. If ever you are in doubt about what foods and how much to serve, consult your veterinarian.

Feeding Requirements

FEEDING GUIDELINES

Some things to bear in mind with regard to your dog's feeding regimen follow.

- Nutritional balance, provided by many commercial dog foods, is vital; avoid feeding a one-sided all-meat diet. Variety in the kinds of meat (beef, lamb, chicken, liver) or cereal grains (wheat, oats, corn) that you offer your dog is of secondary importance compared to the balance or "completeness" of dietary components.
- Always refrigerate opened canned food so that it doesn't spoil. Remember to remove all uneaten portions of canned or moistened food from the feeding dish as soon as the pup has finished his meal. Discard the leftover food immediately and thoroughly wash and dry the feeding dish, as a dirty dish is a breeding ground for harmful germs.
- When offering dry foods, always keep a supply of water on hand for your dog. Water should be made available at all times, even if dry foods are not left out for self-feeding. Each day the water dish should be washed with soap and hot water, rinsed well, and dried; a refill of clean, fresh water should be provided daily.
- Food and water should be served at room temperature, neither too hot nor too cold,

so that it is more palatable for your puppy.

- Serve your pup's meals in sturdy hard-plastic, stainless steel, or earthenware containers, ones that won't tip over as the dog gulps his food down. Some bowls and dishes are weighted to prevent spillage, while others fit neatly into holders which offer support. Feeding dishes should be large enough to hold each meal.
- Whenever the nutritional needs of your dog change— that is to say, when it grows older or if it becomes ill, obese, or pregnant; or if it starts to nurse its young— special diets are in order. Always contact your vet for advice on these special dietary requirements.
- Feed your puppy at the same regular intervals each day; reserve treats for special occasions or, perhaps, to reward good behavior during training sessions.
- Hard foods, such as biscuits and dog meal, should be offered regularly. Chewing on these hard, dry morsels helps the dog keep its teeth clean and its gums conditioned.
- Never overfeed your dog. If given the chance, he will accept and relish every in-between-meal tidbit you offer him. This pampering will only put extra weight on your pet

Made from 89% digestible cheese protein, this Chooz™ treat is purported to be the most healthy dog chew available. If it's too hard for your dog, simply microwave it for a minute or so and it becomes a crispy, crunchy, delectable dog biscuit. It comes in many sizes.

and cause him to be unhealthy in the long run.
- Do not encourage your dog to beg for food from the table while you are eating your meals.

- Food can be effectively used by the owner to train the dog. Doggie treats are practical and often nutritional—choose your chew treats choosily.

FEEDING CHART

Age and No. of Feedings Per Day	Weight in Lbs.	Weight in Kg.	Caloric Requirement kcal M.E./Day
Puppies—Weaning to 3 months Four per day	1–3 3–6 6–12 12–20 15–30	.5–1.4 1.4–2.7 2.7–5.4 5.4–9.1 6.8–13.6	124–334 334–574 574–943 943–1384 1113–1872
Puppies—3 to 6 months Three per day	3–10 5–15 12–25 20–40 30–70	1.4–4.5 2.3–6.8 5.4–11.3 9.1–18.2 13.6–31.8	334–816 494–1113 943–1645 1384–2352 1872–3542
Puppies—6 to 12 months Two per day	6–12 12–25 20–50 40–70 70–100	2.7–5.4 5.4–11.3 9.1–22.7 18.2–31.8 31.8–45.4	574–943 943–1645 1384–2750 2352–3542 3542–4640
Normally Active Adults One or two per day	6–12 12–25 25–50 50–90 90–175	2.7–5.4 5.4–11.3 11.3–22.7 22.7–40.8 40.8–79.4	286–472 472–823 823–1375 1375–2151 2151–3675

This chart presents general parameters of a dog's caloric requirements, based on weight. The total caloric intake comes from a complete, balanced diet of quality foods. To assist owners, dog food companies generally provide the nutritional information of their product right on the label.

Accommodations

Puppies newly weaned from their mother and siblings should be kept warm at all times. As they get older, they can be acclimated gradually to cooler temperatures. When you purchase your dog, find out from the seller whether he is hardy and can withstand the rigors of outdoor living. Many breeds have been known to adapt well to a surprising number of

invest in a crate for him to call his "home" whenever he needs to be confined for short intervals. You might plan to partition off a special room, or part of a room, for your pooch; or you may find that a heated garage or finished basement works well as your dog's living quarters. If your breed can tolerate living outside, you may want to buy or build him his own dog house with an

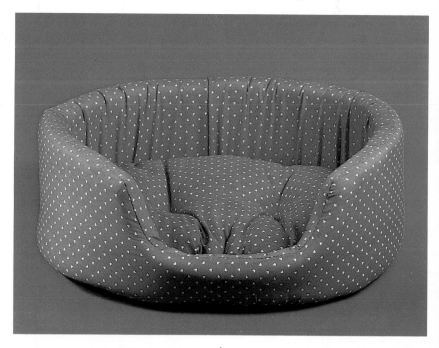

environments, so long as they are given time to adjust. If your pup is to be an indoor companion, perhaps a dog bed in the corner of the family room will suffice; or you may want to

A bed for your dog gives him a place to call his own. His bed should be placed in a warm, dry, draft-free location.

Accommodations

attached run. It might be feasible to place his house in your fenced-in backyard. The breed that can live outdoors fares well when given access to some sort of warm, dry shelter during periods of inclement weather. As you begin thinking about where your canine friend will spend most of his time, you'll want to consider his breed, his age, his temperament, his need for exercise, and the money, space, and resources you have available to house him.

THE DOG BED

In preparing for your puppy's arrival, it is recommended that a dog bed be waiting for him so that he has a place to sleep and rest. If you have provided him with his own bed or basket, ensure that it is placed in a warm, dry, draft-free spot that is private but at the same time near the center of family activity. Refrain from placing his bed near the feed and water dishes or his toilet area. You may want to give your puppy something with

Dog beds come in a variety of sizes and styles and are easily acquired at your local pet shop. Choose one that will accommodate your puppy when he has reached his full-grown size.

Use discretion when giving your dog a toy. Children's toys are not puppies' toys. A pup can easily remove and ingest a button-eye, causing serious complications and even death.

which to snuggle, such as a laundered towel or blanket or an article of old clothing. Some dogs have been known to chew apart their beds and bedding, but you can easily channel this chewing energy into more constructive behavior simply by supplying him with some safe toys or a Nylabone® pacifier for gnawing. Pet shops stock dog beds, among other supplies that you might need for your pup. Select a bed that is roomy, comfortable, and easy to clean, keeping in mind that you may have to replace the smaller bed with a larger one as the puppy grows to adulthood. Remember to clean and disinfect the bed and sleeping area from time to time, as these can become parasitic playgrounds for fleas, lice, mites, and the like.

Accommodations

THE CRATE

Although many dog lovers may cringe at the mere mention of the word *crate,* thinking of it as a cage or a cruel means of confinement, this handy piece of equipment can be put to good use for puppies and grown dogs alike. Even though you may love your dog to an extraordinary degree, you may not want him to have free rein of the house, particularly when you are not home to supervise him. If used properly, a crate can restrict your dog when it is not convenient to have him underfoot, *i.e.,* when guests are visiting or during your mealtimes.

A surprising number of dog owners, who originally had negative feelings about crating their dogs, have had great success using crates. The crate itself serves as a bed, provided it is furnished with bedding material, or it can be used as an indoor dog house. Not all dogs readily accept crates or being confined in them for short intervals, so for these dogs, another means of restriction must be found. But for those dogs that do adjust to spending

Crates allow for safe and easy travel and aid in the housebreaking process. Crates come in a variety of sizes, styles and colors.

time in these structures, the crate can be useful in many ways. The animal can be confined for a few hours while you are away from home or at work, or you can bring your crated dog along with you in the car when you travel or go on vacation. Crates also prove handy as carriers whenever you have to transport a sick dog to the veterinarian.

Most crates are made of sturdy wire or plastic, and some of the collapsible models can be conveniently stored or folded so that they can be moved easily from room to room or from inside the house to the yard on a warm, sunny day. If you allow your puppy or grown dog to become acquainted with its crate by cleverly propping the door open and leaving some of his favorite toys inside, in no time he will come to regard the crate as his own doggie haven. As with a dog bed, place the crate away from drafts in a dry, warm spot; refrain from placing food and water dishes in it, as these only crowd the space and offer opportunity for spillage.

If you need to confine your puppy so that he can't get into mischief while you're not home, remember to consider the animal's needs at all times. Select a large crate, one in which the dog can stand up and move around comfortably; in fact, bigger is better in this context.

The crate you choose for your dog should be appropriately sized. A crate can provide the new pet with a sense of security and belonging. Easily accessible, crates are an inexpensive, sensible investment.

Never leave the animal confined for more than a few hours at a time without letting him out to exercise, play, and, if necessary, relieve himself. Never crate a dog for ten hours, for example, unless you keep the door to the crate open so that he can get out for food and water and to stretch a bit. If long intervals of confinement are necessary, consider placing the unlatched crate in a partitioned section of your house or apartment.

Crates have become the answer for many a dog owner faced with the dilemma of either

Accommodations

getting rid of a destructive dog or living with him despite his bad habits. People who have neither the time nor the patience to train their dogs, or to modify undesirable behavior patterns, can at least restrain their pets during the times they can't be there to supervise. So long as the crate is used in a humane fashion, whereby a dog is confined for no more than a few hours at any one time, it can figure importantly in a dog owner's life. Show dogs, incidentally, learn at an early age that much time will be spent in and out of crates while they are on the show circuit. Many canine celebrities are kept in their crates until they are called to ringside, and they spend many hours crated to and from the shows.

THE DOG HOUSE

These structures, often made of wood, should be sturdy and

Consider your dog's present and fully grown size before purchasing the proper crate for him.

Commercial dog houses are designed for comfort and pest control.

offer enough room for your dog to stretch out in when it rests or sleeps. Dog houses that are elevated or situated on a platform protect the animal from cold and dampness that may seep through the ground. Of the breeds that are temperature hardy and will live outdoors, some are housed outside during the daytime only; others are permanent outdoor residents day and night, all year 'round.

If your intention is to have a companion that lives out-of-doors, it will be necessary to provide him with a more elaborate house, one that really protects him from the elements. Make sure the dog's house is constructed of waterproof materials. Furnish him with sufficient bedding to burrow into on a chilly night and provide extra insulation to keep out drafts and wet weather. Add a partition (a kind of room divider which separates the entry area from the main sleeping space) inside his house or attach a swinging door to the entrance to help keep him warm when he is inside his residence. The swinging door facilitates entry to and from the dog house, while at the same time it provides protection, particularly from wind and drafts.

Some fortunate owners whose yards are enclosed by high fencing allow their dogs complete freedom within the boundaries of their property. In these situations, a dog can leave his dog house and get all the exercise he wants. Of course such a large space requires more effort to keep it clean. An alternative to complete backyard freedom is a dog kennel or run which attaches to or surrounds the dog's house. This restricts some forms of movement, such as running, perhaps, but it does provide ample room for walking, climbing, jumping, and stretching. Another option is to fence off part of the yard and place the dog house in the enclosure. If you need to tether your dog to its house, make certain to use a fairly long lead so as not to hamper the animal's need to move and exercise his limbs.

A thick drape hung over the entrance to the dog's house will prevent drafts, thus keeping your dog warm and dry.

CLEANLINESS

No matter where your dog lives, either in or out of your home, be sure to keep him in surroundings that are as clean and sanitary as possible. His excrement should be removed and disposed of every day without fail. No dog should be forced to lie in his own feces. If your dog lives in his own house, the floor should be swept occasionally and the bedding should be changed regularly if it becomes soiled. Food and water dishes need to be scrubbed with hot water and detergent and rinsed well to remove all traces of soap. The water dish should be refilled with a supply of fresh water. The dog and his environment must be kept free of parasites (especially fleas and mosquitoes, which can carry disease) with products designed to keep these pests under control. Dog crates need frequent scrubbing, too, as do the floors of kennels and runs. Your pet must be kept clean and comfortable at all times; if you exercise strict sanitary control, you will keep disease and parasite infestation to a minimum.

Just as grooming and bathing keep your dog in a healthy condition, regular cleaning and disinfecting of his living area are important for his overall health. Many dogs that suffer from depression are subjected to

More and more cities and towns are requiring dog owners to clean up after their pets. Commercial pooper scoopers can make the clean-up easy and efficient. They are also helpful for backyard sanitation.

poorly maintained quarters. Your dog's physical and psychological well being are closely related. A clean dog is a healthy and happy dog.

Accommodations

EXERCISE

A well-balanced diet and regular medical attention from a qualified veterinarian are essential in promoting good health for your dog, but so is daily exercise to keep him fit and mentally alert. Dogs that have been confined all day while their owners are at work or school need special attention. There should be some time set aside make this daily ritual more pleasant both for themselves and their canine companions by combining the walk with a little "roughhousing," that is to say, a bit of fun and togetherness.

Whenever possible, take a stroll to an empty lot, a playground, or a nearby park. Attach a long lead to your dog's collar, and let him run and jump and tone his body through

Large outdoor pens are used by many breeding, boarding, and medical professionals. Always inspect the facility before leaving your dog in any professional's care.

each day for play—a romp with a family member, perhaps. Not everyone is lucky enough to let his dog run through an open meadow or along a sandy beach, but even a ten-minute walk in the fresh air will do. Dogs that are house-bound, particularly those that live in apartments, need to be walked out-of-doors after each meal so that they can relieve themselves. Owners can aerobic activity. This will help him burn calories and will keep him trim, and it will also help relieve tension and stress that may have had a chance to develop while you were away all day. For people who work Monday through Friday, weekend jaunts can be especially beneficial, since there will be more time to spend with your canine friend. You might

Responsible breeding practices, regular exercise, and proper nutrition all contribute to sound bone development.

want to engage him in a simple game of fetch with a stick or a rubber ball. Even such basic tricks as rolling over, standing on the hindlegs, or jumping up (all of which can be done inside the home as well) can provide additional exercise. But if you plan to challenge your dog with a real workout to raise his heart rate, remember not to push him too hard without first warming up with a brisk walk. Don't forget to "cool him down" afterwards with a rhythmic trot until his heart rate returns to normal. Some dog owners jog with their dogs or take them along on bicycle excursions.

At the very least, however, play with your dog every day to keep him in good shape physically and mentally. If you can walk him outdoors, or better yet run with him in a more vigorous activity, by all means do it. Don't neglect your pet and leave him confined

The knee joint is also known as the stifle joint. It is formed by the articulation of the upper and lower leg.

for long periods without attention from you or time for exercise.

EXERCISING FOR YOU AND YOUR DOG

Dogs are like people. They come in three weights: overweight, underweight, and the correct weight. It is fair to say that most dogs are in better shape than most humans who own them. The reason for this is that most dogs accept exercise without objection—people do not! Follow your dog's lead towards exercise and the complete enjoyment of the outdoors—your dog is the ideal work-out partner. There are toys at your local pet shop which are designed just for that purpose: to allow you to play and exercise with your dog. Here are a few recommended exercise toys for you and your dog.

Flying discs can make exercise exciting.

Frisbee® Flying Discs*

Who hasn't seen or heard of a Frisbee® flying disc? This flying-saucer–like toy is available in three or more sizes. The small size is 10 cm (4″); the medium size is about 15 cm (6″) and the larger size is 23 cm (9″). The size of the flying disc has little to do with the size of the dog—small puppies chase anything; some larger dogs chase nothing. The advantage of the larger disc is that it is the same size as the toy made for humans only! Start with the size that you think is best suited for your dog. What is much more important is the material from which the flying disc is made; *soft un-chew-worthy plastic flying discs are not good for dogs.*

Most people play with these polyethylene discs and use these same discs to play with their dogs. Polyethylene plastic discs usually last an hour or so. Every time the dog grabs it, his teeth dig into the cheap plastic, leaving an imprint. In a short while the disc is not useable—and even worse, it may be dangerous, since the dog can break off a chunk and swallow it, or the distorted disc can swerve out of control and hit someone.

*Frisbee® is a trademark of the Kransco Company, California, and is used for their brand of flying disc.

Be sure that you do not throw the flying disc where your dog can injure himself. Open spaces where cars are not permitted or a park are most ideal.

Nylon Discs

Your pet shop will have a nylon disc that has a dog bone molded into the top of it. While this may look silly at first, the advantage is simple. When a typical Frisbee® lands on a flat surface, the dog may be unable to grasp it with its mouth or turn it over with its paw. Thus frustrated, the dog loses interest in the game and you will have to fetch it yourself. The nylon disc with the bone molded into the top of it allows the dog the option of flipping it over with its paw or grasping it with its mouth. It also has more capacity; thus you can use it as a food or water dish on these outings. The nylon disc may also be flavored and scented, besides being annealed, so your dog can find it more easily if it gets lost in the woods or high grass.

Accommodations

Polyurethane Flexible Floppy Flying Discs

The greatest advance in flying discs came with the manufacture of these discs from polyurethane. The polyurethane is so soft that it doesn't hurt you, your dog, or the window it might strike accidentally. Only very, very rarely can it break a window—usually one that was already cracked. The polyurethane Gumadisc® is floppy and soft. It can be folded

Gumabone® flying discs are proven safe and durable for dogs. The soft, pliable texture and the scent impregnation make these discs loved by dogs.

and fits into your pocket. It is also much tougher than cheap plastics, and most pet shops guarantee that it will last ten times longer than cheap plastic discs.

With most flying discs made for dogs comes an instruction booklet on how to use the disc with your canine friend. Basically, you play with the dog and the disc so the dog knows the disc belongs to him. Then you throw it continuously, increasing the distance, so that the dog fetches it and brings it back to you.

The exercise for you comes in when your dog stops fetching it, or when you have a partner. The two of you play catch. You stand as far apart as available space allows—usually 30–35 m (100 feet) is more than enough room. You throw the disc to each other, arousing your dog's interest as he tries to catch it. When the disc is dropped or veers off, the dog grabs it and brings it back (hopefully). Obviously you will have to run to catch the disc before your dog does.

There are contests held all over the world where distance, height, and other characteristics are measured competitively. Ask your local pet shop to help you locate a Frisbee® Club near you.

*Frisbee® is a trademark of the Kransco Company, California, and is used for their brand of flying disc.

Many owners complain that plastic flying discs are destroyed quickly by their dogs, making an otherwise fun pastime an expensive outing. Flying discs made of annealed nylon are proven to last longer and thereby provide hours of enjoyable, affordable exercise for you and your dog.

Tug Toys

A tug toy is a hard rubber, cheap plastic, or polyurethane toy which allows a dog and his owner to have a game of tug-o-war. The owner grips one end while the dog grips the other—then they pull. The polyurethane flexible tug toy is the best on the market at the present time. Your pet shop will have one to show you. The polyurethane toys are clear in color and stay soft forever. Cheap plastic tug toys are indisputably dangerous, and the hard-rubber tug toys get brittle too fast and are too stiff for most dogs; however, there *is* a difference in price—just ask the advice of any shop operator.

Most every dog loves a challenging tug of war. Tug toys of sturdy polyurethane and strong cotton floss are favorites of many dogs.

Balls made of annealed nylon make fetching safe, pleasing and hygienic for your dog. Their virtually indestructible construction prevents the dog from tearing pieces of the ball and ingesting them, and the appealing scent inspires an enthusiastic retrieve. When worn, as shown here, nylon balls should be replaced with new ones.

Balls

Nobody has to tell you about playing ball with your dog. The reminder you may need is that you should not throw the ball where traffic might interfere with the dog's catching or fetching of it. The ball should not be cheap plastic (a dog's worst enemy as far as toys are concerned) but made of a substantial material. Balls made of nylon are practically indestructible, but they are very hard and must be rolled, never thrown. The same balls made of polyurethane are great—they bounce and are soft. The Nylabone® and Gumabone® balls are scented and flavored, and dogs can easily find them when lost.

Other manufacturers make balls of almost every substance, including plastic, cotton, and wood. Billiard balls, baseballs, tennis balls, and so on, have all been used by dog owners who want their dogs to play with them in a game of catch. A strong caveat is that you use only those balls made especially for dogs.

With the variety of safe, exercise-oriented chew products available, there is little excuse for a sedentary, plaque-infested existence to persist in an otherwise healthy dog.

Housebreaking and Training

Housebreaking can be the groundwork on which all future training is based. The two most commonly recommended methods involve paper training and crate training. When paper training is used, owners often employ litter boxes lined with paper to limit the area and make clean-up fast and easy.

HOUSEBREAKING

The new addition to your family may already have received some basic house training before his arrival in your home. If he has not, remember that a puppy will want to relieve himself about half a dozen times a day; it is up to you to specify where and when he should "do his business." Housebreaking is your first training concern and should begin the moment you bring the puppy home.

Ideally, puppies should be taken outdoors after meals, as a full stomach will exert pressure on the bladder and colon. What goes into the dog must eventually come out; the period after his meal is the most natural and appropriate time. When he eliminates, he should be praised, for this will increase the likelihood of the same thing happening after every meal. He should also be encouraged to use the same area and will probably be attracted to it after frequent use.

Some veterinarians maintain that a puppy can learn to urinate and defecate on command, if properly trained. The advantage of this conditioning technique is that your pet will associate the act of elimination with a particular word of your choice rather than with a particular time or place which might not always be convenient or available. So whether you are visiting an unfamiliar place or don't want to go outside with your dog in sub-zero temperatures, he will still be able to relieve himself when he hears the specific command word. Elimination will occur after this "trigger" phrase or word sets up a conditioned reflex in the dog, who will eliminate anything contained in his bladder or bowel upon hearing it. The shorter the word, the more you can repeat it and imprint it on your dog's memory.

Your chosen command word should be given simultaneously with the sphincter opening events in order to achieve perfect and rapid conditioning. This is why it is important to familiarize yourself with the tell-tale signs preceding your puppy's elimination process. Then you will be prepared to say the word at the crucial moment. There is usually a sense of urgency on the dog's part; he may follow a sniffing and circling pattern which you will soon recognize. It is important to use the command in his usual area only when you know the puppy

can eliminate, i.e., when his stomach or bladder is full. He will soon learn to associate the act with the word. One word of advice, however, if you plan to try out this method: never use the puppy's name or any other word which he might frequently hear about the house—you can imagine the result!

Finally, remember that any training takes time. Such a conditioned response can be obtained with intensive practice with any normal, healthy dog over six weeks of age. Even Pavlov's salivating dogs required fifty repetitions before the desired response was achieved. Patience and persistence will eventually produce results—do not lose heart!

Indoors, sheets of newspapers can be used to cover the specific area where your dog should relieve himself. These should be placed some distance away from his sleeping and feeding area, as a puppy will not urinate or defecate where he eats. When the newspapers are changed, the bottom papers should be placed on top of the new ones in order to reinforce the purpose of the papers by scent as well as by sight. The puppy should be praised during or immediately after he has made use of this particular part of the room. Each positive reinforcement increases the possibility of his using that area again.

When he arrives, it is advisable to limit the puppy to one room, usually the kitchen, as it most likely has a linoleum or easily washable floor surface. Given the run of the house, the sheer size of the place will seem overwhelming and confusing and he might leave his "signature"

PATIENCE, PERSISTENCE, AND PRAISE

As with a human baby, you must be patient, tolerant, and understanding of your pet's mistakes, making him feel loved and wanted, not rejected and isolated. You wouldn't hit a baby for soiling his diapers, as you

An anchored lead can be the solution to a yard without a fence.

on your furniture or clothes! There will be time later to familiarize him gradually with his new surroundings.

would realize that he was not yet able to control his bowel movements; be as compassionate with your canine infant. Never rub his nose in his excreta. Never indulge in the common practice of punishing him with a rolled-up newspaper. Never hit a puppy with your hand. He will only become "hand-shy" and learn to fear you. Usually the punishment is meted out sometime after the offense and loses its efficacy, as the bewildered dog cannot connect the two events. Moreover, by association, he will soon learn to be afraid of you and anything to do with newspapers—including, perhaps, that area where he is *supposed* to relieve himself!

Most puppies are eager to please. Praise, encouragement, and reward (particularly the food

From the moment you bring your dog home, the rules of the house must be enforced to ensure a consistently obedient home companion.

variety) will produce far better results than any scolding or physical punishment. Moreover, it is far better to dissuade your puppy from doing certain things, such as chewing on chair legs or other furniture, by making those objects particularly distasteful to him. Some pet shops stock bitter apple sprays or citronella compounds for application to furniture legs. If these are ineffective, you could smear them with a generous amount of hot chili sauce or cayenne pepper mixed with petroleum jelly, for example. This would make it seem as if the object itself was administering the

Professionals cite that housebreaking on newspapers can cause some dogs to believe that it is always okay to excrete on papers, regardless of location. Housebreaking pads are used by many cautious owners.

punishment whenever he attempted to chew it. He probably wouldn't need a second reminder!

Remember that the reason a dog has housebreaking or behavior problems is because his owner has allowed them to develop. This is why you must begin as you intend to continue, letting your dog know what is acceptable and unacceptable behavior. It is also important that you be consistent in your demands; you cannot feed him from the dining room table one day and then punish him when he begs for food from your dinner guests.

TRAINING

You will want the newest member of your family to be welcomed by everyone; this will not happen if he urinates in every room of the house or barks all night! He needs training in the correct forms of behavior in this new human world. You cannot expect your puppy to become the perfect pet overnight. He needs your help in his socialization process. Training greatly facilitates and enhances the relationship of the dog to his owner and to the rest of society. A successfully trained dog can be taken anywhere and behave well with anyone. Indeed, it is that one crucial word—*training*—which can transform an aggressive animal into a peaceful, well-behaved pet. Now, how does this "transformation" take place?

Some owners of small dogs use a figure-eight-style harness as a means of restraint.

Collars should always be worn, with identification tag and license attached.

WHEN AND HOW TO TRAIN

Like housebreaking, training should begin as soon as the puppy enters the house. The formal training sessions should be short but frequent, for example, ten to fifteen minute periods three times a day. These are much more effective than long, tiring sessions of half an hour which might soon become boring. You are building your relationship with your puppy during these times, so make them as enjoyable as possible. It is a good idea to have these sessions *before* the puppy's meal, not after it when he wouldn't feel like exerting himself; the dog will then associate something pleasurable with his training sessions and look forward to them.

THE COLLAR AND LEASH

Your puppy should become used to a collar and leash as soon as possible. If he is very

The variety of canine collars and leashes available surely allows for the personal touch.

young, a thin, choke-chain collar can be used, but you will need a larger and heavier one for training when he is a little older. Remember to have his name and address on an identification tag attached to his collar, as you don't want to lose your pet if he

A choke collar can be an effective training tool when used properly.

should happen to leave your premises and explore the neighborhood!

Let the puppy wear his collar until he is used to how it feels. After a short time he will soon become accustomed to it and you can attach the leash. He might resist your attempts to lead him or simply sit down and refuse to budge. Fight him for a few minutes, tugging on the leash if necessary, then let him relax for the day. He won't be trained until he learns that he must obey the pull under any circumstance, but this will take a few sessions. Remember that a dog's period of concentration is short, so LITTLE and OFTEN is the wisest course of action—and patience is the password to success.

GIVING COMMANDS

When you begin giving your puppy simple commands, make them as short as possible and use the same word with the same meaning at all times, for example, "Heel," "Sit," and "Stay." You must be consistent; otherwise your puppy will become confused. The dog's name should prefix all commands to attract his attention. Do not become impatient with him however many times you have to repeat your command.

A good way to introduce the "Come" command is by calling the puppy when his meal is ready. Once this is learned, you can call your pet to you at will, always remembering to praise him for his prompt obedience. This "reward," or positive reinforcement, is such a crucial part of training that a Director of the New York Academy of Dog Training constructed his whole teaching program upon the methods of "Love, Praise, and Reward." Incidentally, if you use the command "Come," use it every time. Don't switch to "Come here" or "Come boy," as this will only confuse your dog.

It is worth underlining the fact that punishment is an ineffective teaching technique. We have already seen this in housebreaking. For example, if your pup should run away, it

A puppy's collar should be light and comfortable, yet still effectively secure the dog.

would be senseless to beat him when he eventually returns; he would only connect the punishment with his return, not with running away! In addition, it is unwise to call him to you to punish him, as he will soon learn not to respond when you call his name.

A lead that allows for a sure, comfortable grip is a training necessity. Introduce your new dog to the lead slowly. When he becomes comfortable with it, training can begin.

SOME SPECIFIC COMMANDS

"Sit" This is one of the easiest and most useful commands for your dog to learn, so it is a good idea to begin with it. The only equipment required is a leash, a collar, and a few tasty tidbits. Take your dog out for some exercise before his meal. After about five minutes, call him to you, praise him when he arrives,

A popular item with owners who love to walk their dogs is the harness. The harness fits comfortably around the dog's forequarters and displaces the pressure of the owner's tug on the lead.

and slip his collar on him. Hold the leash tightly in your right hand; this should force the dog's head up and focus his attention on you. As you say "Sit" in a loud, clear voice, with your left hand press steadily on his rump until he is in a sitting position. As soon as he is in the correct position, praise him and give him the tidbit you have in your hand. Now wait a few minutes to let him rest and repeat the routine. Through repetition, the dog soon associates the word with the act. Never make the lesson too long. Eventually your praise will be reward enough for your puppy. Other methods to teach this command exist, but this one, executed with care and moderation, has proven the most effective.

"Sit-Stay/Stay" To teach your pet to remain in one place or "stay" on your command, first of all order him to the sitting position at your side. Lower your left hand with the flat of your palm in front of his nose and your fingers pointing downwards. Hold the leash high and taut behind his head so that he cannot move. Speak the command "Sit-stay" and, as you are giving it, step in front of him. Repeat the command and tighten the leash so the animal cannot follow you. Walk completely around him, repeating the command and keeping him motionless by holding the leash at arm's length above him to check his movement. When he remains in this position for about fifteen seconds, you can begin the second part of the training. You will have to exchange the leash for a nylon cord or rope about twenty to thirty feet long. Repeat the whole routine from the beginning and be ready to prevent any movement towards you with a sharp "Sit-stay." Move around him in ever-widening circles until you are about fifteen feet away from him. If he still remains seated, you can pat yourself on the back! One useful thing to remember is that the dog makes associations with what you say, how you say it, and what you do while you are saying it. Give this command in a firm, clear tone of voice, perhaps using an admonishing forefinger raised, warning the dog to "stay."

Two training accessories especially common with obedience trial enthusiasts are the hurdle (above) and the dumbbell (below). To see dogs performing with these and other field accessories, attend an obedience competition. Remember that training requires consistency and commitment, but the rewards are well worth the effort.

"Heel" When you walk your dog, you should hold the leash firmly in your right hand. The dog should walk on your left so you have the leash crossing your body. This enables you to have greater control over the dog.

Let your dog lead you for the first few moments so that he fully understands that freedom can be his if he goes about it properly. He already knows that when he wants to go outdoors the leash and collar are necessary, so he has respect for the leash. Now, if he starts to pull in one direction while walking, all you do is *stop walking.* He will walk a few steps and then find that he can't walk any further. He will then turn and look into your face. *This is the crucial point!* Just stand there for a moment and stare right back at him . . . now walk another ten feet and stop again. Again your dog will probably walk to the end of the leash, find he can't go any further, and turn around and look again. If he starts to pull and jerk, just stand there. After he quiets down, bend down and comfort him, as he may be frightened. Keep up this training until he learns not to outwalk you.

Once the puppy obeys the pull of the leash, half of your training is accomplished. "Heeling" is a necessity for a well-behaved dog, so teach him to walk beside you, head even with your knee.

Nothing looks sadder than a big dog taking his helpless owner for a walk. It is annoying to passers-by and other dog owners to have a large dog, however friendly, bear down on them and entangle dogs, people, and packages.

To teach your dog, start off walking briskly, saying "Heel" in a firm voice. Pull back with a sharp jerk if he lunges ahead, and if he lags repeat the command and tug on the leash, not allowing him to drag behind. After the dog has learned to heel at various speeds on leash, you

The lead is an essential tool for teaching such commands as "heel," "come," and "down."

can remove it and practice heeling free, but have it ready to snap on again as soon as he wanders.

"Come" Your dog has already learned to come to you when you call his name. Why? Because you only call him when his food is ready or when you wish to play with him or praise him. Outdoors such a response is more difficult to achieve, if he is happily playing by himself or with other dogs, so he must be trained to come to you when he is called. To teach him to come, let him reach the end of a long lead, then give the command, gently pulling him towards you at the same time. As soon as he associates the word *come* with the action of moving towards you, pull only when he does not respond immediately. As he starts to come, move back to make him learn that he must come from a distance as well as when he is close to you. Soon you may be able to practice without a leash, but if he is slow to come or actively disobedient, go to him and pull him toward you, repeating the command. Always remember to reward his successful completion of a task.

"Down" Teaching the "down" command ideally begins while your dog is still a pup. During puppyhood your dog frequently will lie down, as this position is one of the dog's most natural positions. Invest some time, and keep close watch over your pup. Each time he begins to lie, repeat in a low convincing tone the word "down." If for the first day of training, you concur a majority of the dog's sitting with your commands and continue with reinforcement and moderate praise your pup should conquer the "down" command in no time.

Teaching the "down" command to a mature dog likely will require more effort. Although the lying position is still natural to a dog, his being forced into it is not. Some dogs may react with fear, anger, or confusion. Others may accept the process and prove quick learners. Have your

For the dog that responds with anger or aggression, attach a lead (and a muzzle) and have the dog sit facing you at a close distance. There should be a J-loop formed by the lead. With moderate force, relative to the size and strength of your dog, step on the J-loop, forcing the dog down, while repeating the command "down" in a low forceful tone. When the dog is down, moderate praise should

Threats and physical punishment have no place in the canine training process. The keys to effective training are patience, persistence, and praise.

dog sit and face you. If he is responsive and congenial, gently take his paws, and slowly pull them towards you; give the "down" command as he approaches the proper position. Repeat several times: moderate reinforcement of this procedure should prove rewardingly successful.

be given. If the dog proves responsive, you may attempt extending his legs to the "down" position—leaving the muzzle on, of course. Daily reinforcement of the training method will soon yield the desired results. The keys to remember are: patience, persistence, and praise.

Behavior Modification

"Problems with the Barking Dog" and "Aggressive Behavior and Dominance" are extracts from the veterinary monograph *Canine Behavior* (a compilation of columns from *Canine Practice*, a journal published by Veterinary Practice Publishing Company).

PROBLEMS WITH THE BARKING DOG

One of the most frequent complaints about canine behavior is barking. Aside from the biting dog, the barking dog is probably the pet peeve of many non-dog owners. I know of at least one city in which owners of dogs that bark excessively, and for which there are complaints on file, are required to take steps to eliminate the barking.

Canine practitioners are drawn into problems with barking when they are asked for their advice in helping an owner come up with a solution or, as a last resort, when they are requested to perform a debarking operation or even euthanasia. In this column I will deal with some of the factors that apparently cause dogs to bark and suggest some corrective approaches.

Barking is, of course, a natural response for many dogs. They have an inherited predisposition to bark as an alarm when other dogs or people approach their territory. Alarm barking makes

A problem facing many dog owners is excessive vocalization. Fortunately, a number of correctives have proven successful.

many dogs valuable as household watchdogs and is not necessarily undesirable behavior. With a different vocal tone and pattern, dogs bark when they are playing with each other. On occasion dogs have a tendency to bark back at other dogs or join in with other barking dogs.

In addition to inherited barking tendencies, dogs can also learn to bark if the barking is followed, at least sometimes, by a reward. Thus dogs may bark when they wish to come in the house or to get out of a kennel. Some dogs are trained to bark upon hearing the command "speak" for a food reward.

One of the first approaches to

101

take when discussing a barking problem is to determine if the behavior is a manifestation of a natural (inherited) tendency or is learned behavior which has been rewarded in the past.

Can Barking Be Extinguished?

Extinction, as a way of eliminating a behavioral problem, may be considered when it is clear that the behavior has been learned and when one can identify the specific rewarding or reinforcing factors that maintain the behavior.

For example, the dog that barks upon hearing the command "speak" is periodically rewarded with food and praise. If a dog is never, ever given food or praise again when it barks after being told to "speak," it will eventually stop this type of barking. This is the process of extinction and it implies that the

Reward in the form of treats is often effective.

behavior must be repeated but never again rewarded.

A more practical example of the possible use of extinction would be in dealing with the dog that apparently barks because, at least occasionally, it is allowed in the house. By not allowing the dog in the house until the barking has become very frequent and loud, the owners may have shaped the barking behavior to that which is the most objectionable. If the dog is never allowed in the house again when barking, the barking should eventually be extinguished—at least theoretically.

How Should Punishment Be Used?

Sometimes it is not feasible to attempt to extinguish barking even if it seems to be the case that the behavior was learned. This brings up the advisability of punishment. Clients who seek advice in dealing with a barking problem may already have employed some type of punishment such as shouting at the dog or throwing something at it. That this type of punishment is ineffective is attested to by the fact that the client is seeking advice. By shouting at a dog or hitting, a person interferes with what effect the punishment may have on the behavior itself through the arousal of autonomic reactions and escape attempts or submissive responses by the dog.

The Water Bucket Approach

I am rather impressed by the ingenuity of some dog owners in coming up with ways to punish a dog for barking without being directly involved in administering the punishment. One such harried dog owner I talked to, who was also a veterinarian, was plagued by his dog's barking in the kennel commencing at about 1:30 a.m. every night. A platform to hold a bucket of water was constructed over the area of the kennel in which the dog usually chose to bark. Through a system of hinges, ropes, and pulleys, a mechanism was devised so that the dog owner could pull a rope from his bedroom window, dumping a bucket of water on the dog when he started to bark. The bucket was suspended such that once it was dumped, it uprighted itself and the owner could fill it again remotely by turning on a garden hose. After two appropriate dunkings, the dog's barking behavior was apparently eliminated.

With a little ingenuity, a bucket attached to a trap door can be constructed. Soaking the dog in this surprising manner can possibly extinguish a bad barking habit. Always take into consideration the weather conditions, the health and age of your dog, and the cause of the barking problem before embarking on the water-bucket cure.

In advising a client on the type of punishment discussed above, keep in mind one important consideration. From the time the owner is ready to administer punishment for barking, every attempt should be made to punish all undesirable barking from that point on and not to allow excessively long periods of barking to go unpunished. Thus it may be necessary to keep a dog indoors when away unless the dog will be punished for barking when the owner is gone.

Behavior Modification

Alternative Responses Barking dogs are, and probably always will be, one of the enduring problems of dog owners. Barking is relatively effortless, and it is such a natural response for many dogs that it is admittedly hard to eliminate with either punishment or a program of conditioning non-barking. In some instances it may be advisable to forget about eliminating barking and to suggest that the problem be dealt with by changing the circumstances which lead to barking. For example, a dog that barks continuously in the backyard while the owners are away may not bark if left in the house while they are gone. But the problem of keeping the dog in the house may be related to inadequate house training or the dog's shedding hair or climbing onto the furniture. It may be easier to correct these latter behavioral problems than it is to change the barking behavior.

Especially for aggressive dogs, muzzles can prevent both injuries and lawsuits.

AGGRESSIVE BEHAVIOR AND DOMINANCE

Aggressiveness can have many causes. Determining what kind of aggression an animal is manifesting is a prerequisite to successful treatment of the behavior. A frequent problem that is presented to the practitioner is one of aggression related to dominance.

Dogs, which are social animals, have a hierarchal system of dominance within their pack. This predisposition to take a dominant or submissive position relative to fellow canines also occurs in relationship to people. Only in unusual situations would a submissive dog threaten a dominant animal, and almost never would it physically assault its superior. The dominant dog, however, frequently threatens submissive individuals to maintain its position. In a household setting, a person may be the object of threats, and when the person backs off, the dog's position is reassured. The aggressive behavior is also reinforced, and when behavior is reinforced it is likely to recur.

Case History The following is a typical case history of a dog presented for aggression stemming from dominance.

Max was a two-year-old intact male Cocker Spaniel. He had been acquired by Mr. Smith, one year prior to his owner's marriage, as a puppy. He liked and was well liked by both Mr. and Mrs. Smith. He frequently solicited and received attention from both people. However, several times over the last few months, Max had snapped at Mrs. Smith and repeatedly growled at her. A detailed anamnesis revealed that such incidents usually occurred in situations where the dog wanted his own way or did not want to be bothered. He would growl if asked to move off a chair or if persistently commanded to do a specific task. He growled if Mrs. Smith came between him and a young female Cocker Spaniel acquired a year ago. He also refused to let Mrs. Smith take anything from his possession.

Behavior Modification

Max never showed any of these aggressive behaviors toward Mr. Smith or strangers. Admittedly he did not have much opportunity to demonstrate such behaviors toward strangers. A description of the dog's body and facial postures and circumstances under which the

Dogs can become possessive of their playthings or aggressive in defense of their territory.

aggression occurred did not indicate that this was a case of fear-induced aggression, but rather one of assertion of dominance.

Mrs. Smith's reaction to the aggression was always to retreat, and, hence, the dog was rewarded for his assertiveness. She had never physically disciplined the dog and was afraid to do so. To encourage her to physically take control of the dog would likely have resulted in her being bitten. The dominance-submissive relationship had to be reversed in a more subtle manner.

Instructions to Client Mrs. Smith was instructed to avoid all situations which might evoke any aggressive signs from Max. This was to prevent any further reinforcement of his growling and threats.

Both she and her husband were not to indiscriminately pet or show affection towards the dog. For the time being, if Max solicited attention from Mr. Smith, he was to ignore the dog. Mrs. Smith was to take advantage of Max's desire for attention by giving him a command which he had to obey before she praised and petted him. She was also to take advantage of high motivation levels for other activities whenever such situations arose. Max had to obey a command before she gave him anything—

before she petted him, before she let him out or in, etc.

Mrs. Smith also was to assume total care of the dog and become "the source of all good things in life" for Max. She was to feed him, take him on walks, play with him, etc.

Mrs. Smith also spent 5–10 minutes a day teaching Max simple parlor tricks and obedience responses for coveted food rewards as well as praise. These were entirely fun and play sessions—but within a few days the dog had acquired the habit of quickly responding to commands. And this habit transferred over to the non-game situations.

Results Within a few weeks,

The dog's bed can become an object of possession. The dog can come to perceive it as his territory, not allowing others to come near. In such instances behavior modification may be necessary.

Max had ceased to growl and threaten Mrs. Smith in situations that he previously had. He would move out of her way or lie quietly when she would pass by him. She could order him off the furniture and handle the female Cocker Spaniel without eliciting threats from Max.

Mrs. Smith still felt that she would not be able to take the objects from Max's possession. Additional instructions were

Behavior Modification

A dog comes to associate the pleasure of receiving a treat with the action immediately preceding it. Treats are effective in shaping behavior and building a relationship with your pet when they are used judiciously and in moderation.

given to her. She then began placing a series of objects at progressively closer distances to the dog while the dog was in a sit-stay position. After she placed the object on the floor for a short time, she would pick it up. If the dog was still in a sit-stay (which it always was), he received a reward of cheese and verbal praise. Eventually the objects were to be placed and removed from directly in front of the dog. At first she was to use objects that the dog did not care much about and then progressively use more coveted items. This was what she was supposed to do, but before she actually had completed the program she called in excitedly to report that she had taken a piece of stolen food and a household ornament from Max's mouth. And he didn't even object! She said she had calmly told Max to sit. He did. He was so used to doing so, in the game and other situations, that the response was now automatic. She walked over, removed the item from his mouth, and praised him.

Mrs. Smith did resume the systematic presentation of objects and put the dog on an intermittent schedule of food and praise reinforcement during the practice sessions. Mr. Smith again began interacting with Max.

A progress check six months later indicated Max was still an obedient dog and had definitely assumed a submissive position relative to both of his owners. The dominance hierarchy between Max and Mrs. Smith had been reversed *without resorting to any physical punishment.* Mrs. Smith was instructed to reinforce her dominance position by frequently giving Max a command and reinforcing him for the appropriate response.

Summary The essential elements in treatment of such cases are as follows. First, of course, there must be a correct diagnosis of what kind of aggressive behavior is occurring. During the course of treatment, the submissive person(s) should avoid all situations that might evoke an aggressive attitude by the dog. All other family members should totally ignore the dog during the treatment interim. The person most dominated by the dog should take over complete care of the dog in addition to spending 5–10 minutes a day teaching the dog tricks or simple obedience commands (sit-stay is a useful one to gain control of the dog in subsequent circumstances). These should be fun-and-games situations. Food rewards are highly recommended in addition to simple praise.

The person submissive to the dog should take the opportunity to give the dog a command, which must be obeyed, before doing anything pleasant for the dog.

It must be emphasized to the owner that no guarantee can be made that the dog will never threaten or be aggressive again. What is being done, as with all other aggression cases, is an attempt to reduce the likelihood, incidence, and intensity of occurrence of the aggressive behavior.

DESTRUCTIVE TENDENCIES

It is ironical but true that a dog's destructive behavior in the home may be proof of his love for his owner. He may be trying to get more attention from his owner or, in other cases, may be expressing his frustration at his owner's absence. An abundance

Some crates have wire-mesh fronts while others do not. The primary consideration in choosing a crate is its ventilation.

Behavior Modification

of unused energy may also contribute to a dog's destructive behavior, and therefore the owner should ensure that his dog has, at least, twenty minutes of vigorous exercise a day.

As a dog's destructive tendencies may stem from his desire to get more attention from his owner, the latter should devote specific periods each day to his dog when he is actively interacting with him. Such a period should contain practice obedience techniques during which the owner can reward the dog with his favorite food as well as praise and affection.

Planned departure conditioning is one specific technique which has been used to solve the problem of destructive tendencies in a puppy. It eventually ensures the dog's good behavior during the owner's absence. A series of

Not just great recreational devices to channel doggie tensions, the Gumabone® products have been scientifically proven to reduce tartar and plaque build-up. These products are available in many shapes and sizes. Gumabone® products should be replaced regularly when they become excessively worn.

short departures, which are identical to real departures, should condition the dog to behave well in the owner's absence. How is this to be achieved? Initially, the departures are so short (2–5 minutes) that the dog has no opportunity to be destructive. The dog is always rewarded for having been good when the owner returns. Gradually the duration of the departures is increased. The departure time is also varied so that the dog does not know when the owner is going to return. Since a different kind of behavior is now expected, it is best if a new stimulus or "atmosphere" is introduced into the training sessions to permit the dog to distinguish these departures as different from previous departures when he was destructive.

This new stimulus could be the sound of the radio or television. The association which the dog will develop is that whenever the "signal" or "stimulus" is on, the owner will return in an unknown

A safe tug toy.

period of time and, if the dog has not been destructive, he will be rewarded. As with the daily owner-dog interaction, the food reward is especially useful.

If the dog misbehaves during his owner's absence, the owner should speak sternly to him and isolate him from social contact for at least thirty minutes. (Puppies hate to be ignored.) Then the owner should conduct another departure of a shorter time and generously reward good behavior when he returns. The owner should progress slowly enough in the program so that once the departure has been initiated, the dog is never given an opportunity to make a mistake.

If planned departures are working satisfactorily, the departure time may gradually be extended to several hours. To reduce the dog's anxiety when left alone, he should be given a "safety valve" such as the indestructible Nylabone® to play with and chew on.

A proven safe chew product.

Health Care

From the moment you purchase your puppy, the most important person in both your lives becomes your veterinarian. His professional advice and treatment will ensure the good health of your pet. The vet is the first person to call when illness or accidents occur. Do *not* try to be your own veterinarian or apply human remedies to canine diseases. However, just as you would keep a first aid kit handy for minor injuries sustained by members of your family at home, so you should keep a similar kit prepared for your pet.

First aid for your dog would consist of stopping any bleeding, cleaning the wound, and

Even in your own back yard, injuries can occur.

preventing infection. Thus your kit might contain medicated powder, gauze bandages, and adhesive tape to be used in case of cuts. If the cut is deep and bleeding profusely, the bandage should be applied very tightly to help in the formation of a clot. A tight bandage should not be kept in place longer than necessary, so take your pet to the veterinarian immediately.

Walking or running on a cut pad prevents the cut from healing. Proper suturing of the cut and regular changing of the bandages should have your pet's wound healed in a week to ten days. A minor cut should be covered with a light bandage, for you want as much air as possible to reach the wound. Do not apply wads of cotton to a wound; they will stick to the area and may cause contamination.

You should also keep some hydrogen peroxide available, as it is useful in cleaning wounds and is also one of the best and simplest emetics known. Cotton applicator swabs are useful for applying ointment or removing debris from the eyes. A pair of tweezers should also be kept handy for removing foreign bodies from the dog's neck, head or body.

Nearly everything a dog might contract in the way of sickness has basically the same set of symptoms: loss of appetite, diarrhea, dull eyes, dull coat,

When emergencies occur, it pays to be prepared. A first-aid kit, well stocked with common sense medical accessories and tools, is helpful to have available at all times.

warm and/or runny nose, and a high temperature. Therefore, it is most important to take his temperature at the first sign of illness. To do this, you will need a rectal thermometer which should be lubricated with petroleum jelly. Carefully insert it into the rectum, holding it in place for at least two minutes. It must be held firmly; otherwise there is the danger of its being sucked up into the rectum or slipping out, thus giving an inaccurate reading. The normal temperature for a dog is between 101° and 102.5°F. If your pet is seriously ill or injured in an accident, your veterinarian will advise you what to do before he arrives.

SWALLOWING FOREIGN OBJECTS

Most of us have had experience with a child swallowing a foreign object. Usually it is a small coin; occasionally it may be a fruit pit or something more dangerous. Dogs, *as a general rule,* will not swallow anything which isn't edible. There are, however, many dogs that swallow pebbles or small shiny objects such as pins, coins, and bits of cloth and plastic. This is especially true of dogs that are offered so-called "chew toys."

Chew toys are available in many sizes, shapes, colors and materials. Some even have whistles which sound when the dog's owner plays with it or when the dog chomps on it quickly. Most dogs attack the whistle first, doing everything possible to make it stop squeaking. Obviously, if the whistle is made of metal, a dog can injure its mouth, teeth, or tongue. Therefore, *never* buy a "squeak toy" made with a metal whistle.

Other chew toys are made of vinyl, a cheap plastic which is soft to the touch and pliable. Most of the cute little toys that are figures of animals or people are made of this cheap plastic. They are sometimes hand-painted in countries where the cost of such labor is low. Not only is the paint used dangerous to dogs, because of the lead content, but the vinyl tears easily and is usually destroyed by the dog during the first hour. Small bits of vinyl may be ingested and cause blockage of the intestines. You are, therefore, reminded of these things before you buy anything vinyl for your dog!

Very inexpensive dog toys, usually found in supermarkets and other low-price venues, may be made of polyethylene. These are to be avoided completely, as this cheap plastic is, for some odd reason, attractive to dogs. Dogs destroy the toy in minutes and sometimes swallow the indigestible bits and pieces that come off. Most pet shops carry only safe toys.

WHAT TOYS ARE SAFE FOR DOGS?

Hard Rubber Toys made of hard rubber are usually safe for dogs, providing the toy is made of 100% hard rubber and not a compound of rubber and other materials. The rubber must be "virgin" and not re-ground from old tires, tubes, and other scrap rubber products. The main problem with rubber, even 100% virgin rubber, is that it oxidizes quickly, especially when subjected to the ultraviolet rays of the sun and a dog's saliva. The rubber then tends to be brittle, to crack, to dust off, and to be extremely dangerous to dogs that like swallowing things.

From top to bottom, *the four common bite types are: (a) level, (b) scissors, (c) undershot, and (d) overshot. Different breeds have different bite types and one bite type may be desirable in your breed and most undesirable in another.*

Nylon Toys Toys made of nylon could well be the safest of all toys, *providing the nylon is annealed.* Nylon that is not annealed is very fragile ,and if you smash it against a hard surface, it might shatter like glass. The same is true when the weather is cold and the nylon drops below freezing. Thus far there is only one line of dog toys that is made of annealed virgin nylon—Nylabone®. These toys are not only annealed but they are flavored and scented. The flavors and scents, such as hambone, are undetectable by humans, but dogs seem to find them attractive.

Some nylon bones have the flavor sprayed on them or molded into them. These cheaper bones are easy to detect—just smell them. If you discern an odor, you know they are poorly made. The main

The inherent need to chew is strong in dogs of all ages. The canine's constant chewing of his favorite chew products will necessitate their regular replacement. When a bone becomes frayed, it's time to replace it.

problem with the nylon toys that have an odor is that they are not annealed and they "smell up" the house or car. The dog's saliva dilutes the odor of the bone, and when he drops it on your rug, this odor attaches itself to the rug and is quite difficult to remove.

Annealed nylon may be the best there is ,but it is not 100% safe. The Nylabone® dog chews are really meant to be Pooch Pacifiers®. This trade name indicates the effect intended for the dog, which is to relieve the tension in your excited puppy or adult dog who is left alone or wants to "spite" you. Instead of chewing up the furniture or some other object, he chews up his Nylabone® instead. Many dogs ignore the Nylabone® for weeks, suddenly attacking it when they have to relieve their doggie tensions.

Some dogs may have jaws strong enough to chomp off a piece of Nylabone®, but this is extremely rare. *One word of caution:* the Nylabone® should be replaced when the dog has chewed down the knuckle. Most dogs slowly scrape off small slivers of nylon which pass harmlessly through their digestive tract. The resultant frizzled bone actually becomes a toothbrush.

One of the great characteristics of nylon bones is that they can be boiled and

The Gumaknot® is the favorite chew item of many dogs.

Above: *The Nylabone® is an effective, proven-safe therapeutic device.* **Below**: *The Gumaball® is useful for outside recreation, exercise, and tooth care.*

Doggie treats come in a wide variety of sizes, shapes, and flavors. While they can be useful as rewards and occasional tidbits, they do not satisfy the dog's need to chew. Treats are best used for what they are intended—as treats.

sterilized. If a dog loses interest in his Nylabone®, or it is too hard for him to chew due to his age and the condition of his teeth, you can cook it in some chicken or beef broth, allowing it to boil for 30 minutes. Let it cool down normally. It will then be perfectly sterile and re-flavored for the next dog. *Don't try this with plastic bones, as they will melt and ruin your pot.*

Polyurethane Toys Toys made of polyurethane are almost as good as nylon bones—but not quite. There are several brands on the market: ignore the ones which have scents that you can discern. Some of the scented polyurethane bones have an unbearable odor after the scent has rubbed off the bone and onto your rug or car seat. Again, look for the better-quality polyurethane toy. Gumabone® is

a flexible material, the same as used for making artificial hearts and the bumpers on automobiles, thus it is strong and stable. It is not as strong as Nylabone®, but many dogs like it because it is soft.

The most popular of the Gumabone® products made in polyurethane are the tug toys, balls, and Frisbee® flying discs. These items are almost clear in color, have the decided advantage of lasting a long time, and are useful in providing exercise for both a dog and his master or mistress.

Whatever dog toy you buy, be sure it is high quality. Pet shops, as a rule, carry the better-quality toys, while supermarkets seem to be concerned only with price. Of course there may be exceptions, but you are best advised to ask your local pet shop operator—or even your veterinarian—what toys are suitable for *your* dog.

In conclusion, if your dog is a swallower of foreign objects, don't give him anything cheap to chew on. If he swallows a coin, you can hardly blame the Treasury! Unless your dog is carefully supervised, use only the largest size Nylabone®, and replace it as soon as the dog chews down the knuckles. *Do not let the dog take the Nylabone® outdoors.* First of all he can hide and bury it, digging it up when his tensions rise. Then, too, all nylon becomes more brittle when it freezes, even Nylabone®.

IF YOUR PET SWALLOWS POISON

A poisoned dog must be treated instantly; any delay could cause his death. Different poisons act in different ways and require different treatments. If you know the dog has swallowed an acid, alkali, gasoline, or kerosene, do not induce vomiting. Give milk to dilute the poison and rush him to the vet. If you can find the bottle or container of poison, check the label to see if there is a recommended antidote. If not, try to induce vomiting by giving him a mixture of hydrogen peroxide and water. Mix the regular drugstore strength of hydrogen peroxide (3%) with an equal part of water, but do not attempt to pour it down your dog's throat, as that could cause inhalation pneumonia. Instead, simply pull the dog's lips away from the side of his mouth, making a pocket for depositing the liquid. Use at least a tablespoonful of the mixture for every ten pounds of your dog's

Handling a dog who is sick or injured requires skill. To protect yourself from being bitten, you should first secure the dog's muzzle with a slow, cautious motion, if no safety muzzle is available. Then the animal can be treated or transported as required.

weight. He will vomit in about two minutes. When his stomach has settled, give him a teaspoonful of Epsom salts in a little water to empty the intestine quickly. The hydrogen peroxide, on ingestion, becomes oxygen and water and is harmless to your dog; it is the best antidote for phosphorus, which is often used in rat poisons. After you have administered this emergency treatment to your pet and his stomach and bowels have been emptied, rush him to your veterinarian for further care.

DANGER IN THE HOME

There are numerous household products that can prove fatal if ingested by your pet. These include rat poison, antifreeze, boric acid, hand soap, detergents, insecticides, mothballs, household cleansers,

Suburban backyards are often fertile grounds for a variety of flowering plant types. Many of these pretty-to-the-eye plants can be harmful to a canine. Lily-of-the-valley is attractive and popular in some climates; it is, however, poisonous if ingested and should not be cultivated near the dog's living area.

Water hemlock is one of the many poisonous plants that can cause serious complications if ingested by a canine.

bleaches, de-icers, polishes and disinfectants, paint and varnish removers, acetone, turpentine, and even health and beauty aids if ingested in large enough quantities. A word to the wise should be sufficient: what you would keep locked away from your two-year-old child should also be kept hidden from your pet.

There is another danger lurking within the home among the household plants, which are almost all poisonous, even if swallowed in small quantities. There are hundreds of poisonous plants around us, among which are: ivy leaves, cyclamen, lily of the valley, rhododendrons, tulip bulbs, azalea, wisteria, poinsettia

Lactrodectus mactans, better known as the black widow spider, is said to possess venom over 15 times as toxic as many rattlesnakes'. This spider most commonly occurs in warm climates. Owners are encouraged to inspect the dog's living area periodically for such lethal inhabitants.

leaves, mistletoe, daffodils, delphiniums, foxglove leaves, the jimson weed—we cannot name them all. Rhubarb leaves, for example, either raw or cooked, can cause death or violent convulsions. Peach, elderberry, and cherry trees can cause cyanide poisoning if their bark is consumed.

There are also many insects that can be poisonous to dogs such as spiders, bees, wasps, and some flies. A few toads and frogs exude a fluid that can make a dog foam at the mouth—and even kill him—if he bites too hard!

There have been cases of dogs suffering nicotine poisoning by consuming the contents of full ashtrays which thoughtless smokers have left on the coffee table. Also, do not leave nails, staples, pins, or other sharp objects lying around. Likewise, don't let your puppy play with plastic bags which could suffocate him. Unplug, remove, or cover any electrical cords or wires near your dog. Chewing live wires could lead to severe mouth burns or death. Remember that an ounce of prevention is worth a pound of cure: keep all potentially dangerous objects out of your pet's reach.

Bufo marinus, *the giant toad, is a very large species of toad that, when provoked, will produce a secretion that is toxic if ingested. The giant toad can potentially be a canine killer.*

VEHICLE TRAVEL SAFETY

A dog should never be left alone in a car. It takes only a few minutes for the heat to become unbearable in the summer, and to drop to freezing in the winter.

A dog traveling in a car or truck should be well behaved. An undisciplined dog can be deadly in a moving vehicle. The dog should be trained to lie on the back seat of the vehicle. Allowing your dog to stick its head out of the window is unwise. The dog may jump or it may get something in its eye. Some manufacturers sell seat belts and car seats designed for dogs.

Traveling with your dog in the back of your pick-up truck is an unacceptable notion and dangerous to all involved.

PROTECT YOURSELF FIRST

In almost all first aid situations, the dog is in pain. He may indeed be in shock and not appear to be suffering, until you move him. Then he may bite your hand or resist being helped at all. So if you want to help your dog, help yourself first by tying his mouth closed. To do this, use a piece of strong cloth four inches wide and three feet long, depending on the size of the dog. Make a loop in the middle of the strip and slip it over his nose with the knot under his chin and over the bony part of his nose.

Pull it tight and bring the ends back around his head behind the ears and tie it tightly, ending with a bow knot for quick, easy release. Now you can handle the dog safely. As a dog perspires through his tongue, do not leave the "emergency muzzle" on any longer than necessary.

ADMINISTERING MEDICINE

When you are giving liquid medicine to your dog, it is a good idea to pull the lips away from the side of the mouth, form a lip pocket, and let the liquid trickle past the tongue. Remain at his side, never in front of the dog, as he may cough and spray you with the liquid. Moreover, you must never pour liquid medicine while the victim's tongue is drawn out, as inhalation pneumonia could be the disastrous result.

Medicine in pill form is best administered by forcing the dog's mouth open, holding his head back, and placing the capsule as far back on his tongue as you can reach. To do this: put the palm of your hand over the dog's muzzle (his foreface) with your fingers on one side of his jaw, your thumb

An injured dog can bite, rather unintentionally. A make-shift muzzle can be used in the case of an emergency. A tie or a torn piece of cloth can suffice.

123

To avoid inhalation pneumonia, a syringe placed between the dog's gums can be used when administering liquid medications.

on the other. Press his lips hard against his teeth while using your other hand to pull down his lower jaw. With your two fingers, try to put the pill as far back on the dog's tongue as you can reach. Keep his mouth and nostrils closed and he should be forced to swallow the medicine. As the dog will not be feeling well, stroke his neck to comfort him and to help him swallow his medicine more easily. Do keep an eye on him for a few moments afterward, however, to make certain that he does not spit it out.

IN CASE OF AN ACCIDENT

It is often difficult for you to assess the dog's injuries after a road accident. He may appear normal, but there might be internal hemorrhaging. A vital organ could be damaged or ribs broken. Keep the dog as quiet and warm as possible; cover him with blankets or your coat to let his own body heat build up. Signs of shock are a rapid and weak pulse, glassy-eyed appearance, subnormal temperature, and slow capillary refill time. To determine the last symptom, press firmly against the dog's gums until they turn white. Release and count the number of seconds until the gums return to their normal color. If it is more than 2–3 seconds, the dog may be going into shock. Failure to return to the reddish pink color indicates that the dog may be in serious trouble and needs immediate assistance.

If artificial respiration is required, first open the dog's mouth and check for obstructions; extend his tongue and examine the pharynx. Clear his mouth of mucus and blood and hold the mouth slightly open. Mouth-to-mouth resuscitation involves holding the dog's tongue to the bottom of his mouth with one hand and sealing his nostrils with the other while you blow into his mouth. Watch for his chest to rise with each inflation. Repeat every 5–6 seconds, the equivalent of 10–12 breaths a minute.

If the veterinarian cannot come to you, try to improvise a stretcher to take the dog to him.

To administer pills, simply press the dog's lips against his teeth until he opens his mouth. Then place the pill as far back on the tongue as possible. Now hold the dog's mouth closed and see that the dog has swallowed. Praise him for his cooperation.

Health Care

To carry a puppy, wrap him in a blanket that has been folded into several thicknesses. If he is in shock, it is better to pick him up by holding one hand under his chest, the other under the hindquarters. This will keep him stretched out.

It is always better to roll an injured dog than to try and lift him. If you find him lying beside the road after a car accident, apply a muzzle even if you have to use someone's necktie to make one. Send someone for a blanket and roll him gently onto

Known as Elizabethan collars, these devices can be purchased at a pet store or provided by your veterinarian to prevent the dog from complications resulting from excessive licking or chewing.

it. Two people, one on each side, can make a stretcher out of the blanket and move the dog easily.

If no blanket is available and the injured dog must be moved, try to keep him as flat as possible. So many dogs' backs are broken in car accidents that one must first consider that possibility. However, if he can move his hind legs or tail, his spine is probably not broken. Get medical assistance for him immediately.

It should be mentioned that unfortunate car accidents, which can maim or kill your dog, can be avoided if he is confined at all times either indoors or, if out-of-doors, in a fenced-in yard or

Nightshade (left) and larkspur (right) are two plants that are poisonous when ingested. Many dogs eat small amounts of wild grass, which is often harmless if not sprayed with pesticides; however, the owner must be cautious that poisonous plants are not growing in the grass, for they can be accidentally consumed.

some other protective enclosure. *Never* allow your dog to roam free; even a well-trained dog may, for some unknown reason, dart into the street—and the result could be tragic.

If you need to walk your dog, leash him first so that he will be protected from moving vehicles.

PROTECTING YOUR PET

It is important to watch for any tell-tale signs of illness so that you can spare your pet any unnecessary suffering. Your dog's eyes, for example, should normally be bright and alert, so if the haw is bloodshot or partially covers the eye, it may be a sign of illness or irritation. If your dog has matter in the corners of his eyes, bathe them with a mild eye wash; obtain ointment or eye drops from your veterinarian to treat a chronic condition.

If your dog seems to have something wrong with his ears which causes him to scratch at them or shake his head, cautiously probe the ear with a cotton swab. An accumulation of wax will probably work itself out. Dirt or dried blood, however, is indicative of ear mites or infection and should be treated immediately. Sore ears in the summer, due to insect bites, should be washed with mild soap and water, then covered with a soothing ointment and wrapped in gauze if necessary. Keep your pet away from insects until his ears heal, even if this means confining him indoors.

Health Care

INOCULATIONS

Periodic check-ups by your veterinarian throughout your puppy's life are good health insurance. The person from whom your puppy was purchased should tell you what inoculations your puppy has had and when the next visit to the vet is necessary. You must make certain that your puppy has been vaccinated against the following infectious canine diseases: distemper, canine hepatitis, leptospirosis, rabies, parvovirus, and parainfluenza. Annual "boosters" thereafter provide inexpensive protection for your dog against such serious diseases. Puppies should also be checked for worms at an early age.

DISTEMPER

Young dogs are most susceptible to distemper, although it may affect dogs of all ages. Some signs of the disease are loss of appetite, depression, chills, and fever, as well as a watery discharge from the eyes and nose. Unless treated promptly, the disease goes into advanced stages with infections of the lungs, intestines, and nervous system. Dogs that recover may be impaired with paralysis, convulsions, a twitch, or some other defect, usually spastic in nature. Early inoculations in puppyhood

While the vet is inspecting your dog, secure him around the base of his neck and the tuck of his abdomen.

When a dog's ear is injured, it should be bandaged by a professional. A protective collar should then be secured.

should be followed by an annual booster to help protect against this disease.

CANINE HEPATITIS

The signs of hepatitis are drowsiness, vomiting, loss of appetite, high temperature, and great thirst. These signs may be accompanied by swellings of the head, neck, and abdomen. Vomiting may also occur. This disease strikes quickly, and death may occur in only a few hours. An annual booster shot is needed after the initial series of puppy shots.

LEPTOSPIROSIS

Infection caused by either of two serovars, *canicola* or *copehageni* is usually begun by the dog's licking substances contaminated by the urine or feces of infected animals. Brown rats are the main carriers of *copehageni*. The signs are weakness, vomiting, and a yellowish discoloration of the jaws, teeth, and tongue, caused by an inflammation of the kidneys. A veterinarian can administer the bacterins to protect your dog from this disease. The frequency of the doses is determined by the risk factor involved.

RABIES

This disease of the dog's central nervous system spreads by infectious saliva, which is transmitted by the bite of an infected animal. Of the two main classes of signs, the first is "furious rabies," in which the dog shows a period of melancholy or depression, then irritation, and finally paralysis. The first period can be from a few hours to several days, and during this time the dog is cross and will change his position often, lose his appetite, begin to lick, and bite or swallow foreign objects. During this phase the dog is spasmodically wild and has impulses to run away. The dog acts fearless and bites everything in sight. If he is caged or confined, he will fight at the bars and possibly break teeth or fracture his jaw. His bark becomes a peculiar howl. In the final stage, the animal's lower jaw becomes paralyzed and hangs down. He then walks with a stagger, and saliva drips from his mouth. About four to eight days after the onset of paralysis, the dog dies.

The second class of symptoms is referred to as "dumb rabies" and is characterized by the dog's walking in a bearlike manner with his head down. The lower jaw is paralyzed and the dog is unable to bite. It appears as if he has a bone caught in his throat.

If a dog is bitten by a rabid animal, he probably can be saved if he is taken to a veterinarian in time for a series of injections. After the signs appear, however, no cure is possible. The local health

Rats are the carriers of many diseases, including leptospirosis.

department must be notified in the case of a rabid dog, for he is a danger to all who come near him. As with the other shots each year, an annual rabies inoculation is very important. In many areas, the administration of rabies vaccines for dogs is required by law.

PARVOVIRUS

This relatively new virus is a contagious disease that has spread in almost epidemic proportions throughout certain sections of the United States. It has also appeared in Australia, Canada, and Europe. Canine parvovirus attacks the intestinal tract, white blood cells, and heart muscle. It is believed to spread through dog-to-dog contact, and the specific course of infection seems to come from fecal matter of infected dogs. Overcoming parvovirus is difficult, for it is capable of existing in the environment for many months under varying conditions and temperatures, and it can be transmitted from place to place on the hair and feet of infected dogs, as well as on the clothes and shoes of people.

Vomiting and severe diarrhea, which will appear within five to seven days after the animal has been exposed to the virus, are the initial signs of this disease. At the onset of illness, feces will be light gray or yellow-gray in

It is believed that mice can carry the early-stage deer ticks that may be carriers of the dreaded lyme disease.

color, and the urine might be blood-streaked. Because of the vomiting and severe diarrhea, the dog that has contracted the disease will dehydrate quickly. Depression and loss of appetite, as well as a rise in temperature, can accompany the other symptoms. Death caused by this disease usually occurs within 48 to 72 hours following the appearance of the symptoms. Puppies are hardest hit, and the virus is fatal to 75 percent of puppies that contract it. Death in

Stable fly: a painful bite.

puppies can be within two days of the onset of the illness.

A series of shots administered by a veterinarian is the best preventive measure for canine parvovirus. It is also important to disinfect the area where the dog is housed by using one part sodium hypochlorite solution (household bleach) to thirty parts of water and to keep the dog from coming into contact with the fecal matter of other dogs.

Deer tick: a carrier of lyme.

LYME DISEASE

Known as a bacterial infection, Lyme disease is transmitted by ticks infected with a spirochete known as *Borrelia burgdorferi*. The disease is most often acquired by the parasitic bite of an infected deer tick, *Ixodes dammini*. While the range of symptoms is broad, common warning signs include: rash beginning at the bite and soon extending in a bullseye-targetlike fashion; chills, fever, lack of balance, lethargy, and stiffness; swelling and pain, especially in the joints, possibly leading to arthritis or arthritic conditions; heart problems, weak limbs, facial paralysis, and lack of tactile sensation. Although there is no known cure-all, tetracycline and some other drugs have been prescribed with various degrees of success. If you suspect that your dog has Lyme disease, contact your vet immediately.

PARAINFLUENZA

Parainfluenza, or infectious canine tracheobronchitis, is commonly known as "kennel cough." It is highly contagious, affects the upper respiratory system, and is spread through direct or indirect contact with already diseased dogs. It will readily infect dogs of all ages that have not been vaccinated or that were previously infected. While this condition is definitely one of the serious diseases in dogs, it is self-limiting, usually lasting only two to four weeks. The symptoms are high fever and intense, harsh coughing that brings up mucus. As long as your pet sees your veterinarian immediately, the chances for his complete recovery are excellent.

EXTERNAL PARASITES

A parasite is an animal that lives in or on an organism of another species, known as the host, without contributing to the well-being of the host. The majority of dogs' skin problems are parasitic in nature and an estimated 90% of puppies are born with parasites.

Ticks can cause serious problems to dogs where the latter have access to woods, fields, and vegetation in which large numbers of native mammals live. Ticks are usually found clinging to vegetation and attach themselves to animals

Brown dog tick: a common parasite.

Deer fly: a welt-inducing bite.

passing by. They have eight legs and a heavy shield or shell-like covering on their upper surface. Only by keeping dogs away from tick-infested areas can ticks on dogs be prevented.

The flea is the single most common cause of skin and coat problems in dogs. There are 11,000 kinds of fleas which can transmit specific disorders like tapeworm and heartworm or transport smaller parasites onto your dog. The common tapeworm, for example, requires the flea as an intermediate host for completion of its life cycle.

A female flea can lay hundreds of eggs and these will become adults in less than three weeks. Depending on the temperature

The bite of a single flea can cause an irritation that spreads quickly over the surface of the skin. For flea prevention, the dog and his living quarters should be treated regularly.

and the amount of moisture, large numbers of fleas can attack dogs. The ears of dogs, in particular, can play host to hundreds of fleas.

Fleas can lurk in crevices and cracks, carpets, and bedding for months, so frequent cleaning of your dog's environment is absolutely essential. If he is infected by other dogs, then have him bathed and "dipped," which means that he will be put into water containing a chemical that kills fleas. Your veterinarian will advise which dip to use, and your dog must be bathed for at least twenty minutes. These parasites are tenacious and remarkably agile creatures; fleas have existed since prehistoric times and have been found in arctic as well as tropical climates. Some experts claim that fleas can jump 150 times the length of their bodies; this makes them difficult to catch and kill. Thus, treating your pet for parasites without simultaneously

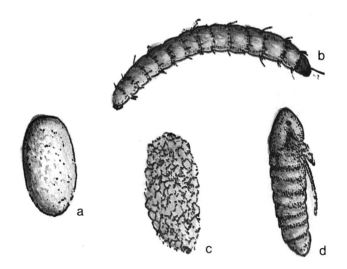

The life cycle of the flea: (a) egg (b) larvae (c) cocoon (d) pupae. If allowed to persist on the dog, fleas will build nests and reproduce, quickly infesting the dog. Regular brushing accompanied by anti-flea applications should suffice to eliminate the flea problem.

treating the environment is both inefficient and ineffective.

INTERNAL PARASITES

Four common internal parasites that may infect a dog are: roundworms, hookworms, whipworms, and tapeworms. The first three can be diagnosed by laboratory examination of the dog's stool, and tapeworms can be seen in the stool or attached to the hair around the anus. When a veterinarian determines what type of worm or worms are present, he then can advise the best treatment.

Roundworms, the dog's most common intestinal parasite, have a life cycle which permits complete eradication by worming twice, ten days apart. The first worming will remove all adults and the second will destroy all subsequently hatched eggs before they, in turn, can produce more parasites.

A dog in good physical condition is less susceptible to worm infestation than a weak dog. Proper sanitation and a nutritious diet help in preventing worms. One of the best preventive measures is to have clean, dry bedding for the dog, as this diminishes the possibility of reinfection due to flea or tick bites.

Heartworm infestation in dogs is passed by mosquitoes. Dogs with this disease tire easily, have difficulty in breathing, and lose weight despite a hearty appetite. Administration of preventive medicine throughout the spring, summer, and fall months is advised. A veterinarian must first take a blood sample from the dog to test for the presence of the disease, and if the dog is heartworm-free, pills or liquid medicine can be prescribed.

Heartworm life cycle: a carrier mosquito bites a dog and deposits microfilariae; the filariae travel through the dog's blood stream, lodging in the heart to reproduce. The carrier dog is later bitten by an uninfected mosquito, which thereby acquires uninfectious microfilariae, develops the microfilariae to an infectious stage, bites and infects another dog.

CANINE SENIOR CITIZENS

The processes of aging and gradual degenerative changes start far earlier in a dog than often observed, usually at about seven years of age. If we recall that each year of a dog's life roughly corresponds to about seven years in the life of a man, by the age of seven he is well into middle age. Your pet will become less active, will have a poorer appetite with increased thirst, there will be frequent periods of constipation and less than normal passage of urine. His skin and coat might become dull and dry and his hair will become thin and fall out. There is a tendency towards obesity in old age, which should be avoided by maintaining a regular exercise program. Remember, also, that your pet will be less able to cope

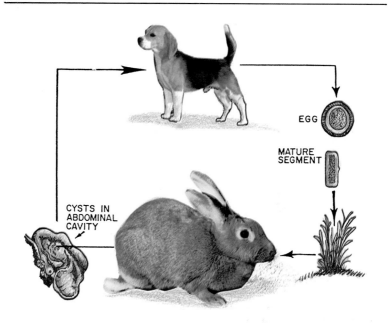

EGG

MATURE SEGMENT

CYSTS IN ABDOMINAL CAVITY

Tapeworms can be acquired in a number of ways; the infected dog must receive veterinary treatment.

with extreme heat, cold, fatigue, and change in routine.

There is the possibility of loss or impairment of hearing or eyesight. He may become bad-tempered more often than in the past. Other ailments such as rheumatism, arthritis, kidney infections, heart disease, male prostatism, and hip dysplasia may occur. Of course, all these require a veterinarian's examination and recommendation of suitable treatment. Care of the teeth is also important in the aging dog.

Indeed, the mouth can be a barometer of nutritional health. Degenerating gums, heavy tartar on the teeth, loose teeth, and sore lips are common. The worst of all diseases in old age, however, is neglect. Good care in early life will have its effect on your dog's later years; the nutrition and general health care of his first few years can determine his lifespan and the quality of his life. It is worth bearing in mind that the older, compared to the younger, animal needs more protein of good biological value, more vitamins A, B-complex, D and E, more calcium and iron, less fat and fewer carbohydrates.

Preventive Dental Care

ALL DOGS NEED TO CHEW

Puppies and young dogs need something with resistance to chew on while their teeth and jaws are developing—to cut the puppy teeth, to induce growth of the permanent teeth under the puppy teeth, to assist in getting rid of the puppy teeth on time, to help the permanent teeth through the gums, to assure normal jaw development and to settle the permanent teeth solidly in the jaws.

The adult dog's desire to chew stems from the instinct for tooth cleaning, gum massage, and jaw exercise—plus the need to vent periodic doggie tensions. . . . A pacifier if you will!

Dental caries, as they affect the teeth of humans, are virtually

It is imperative that the owner take the necessary measures to ensure sound dental health. Ideal canine dentition illustrated: upper palate on right; lower palate on left.

unknown in dogs; but tartar (calculus) accumulates on the teeth of dogs, particularly at the gum line, more rapidly than on the teeth of humans. These accumulations, if not removed, bring irritation and then infection, which erode the tooth enamel and ultimately destroy the teeth at the roots. It is important that you take your dog to your local veterinarian for periodic dental examinations.

Tooth and jaw development will normally continue until the dog is more than a year old—but sometimes much longer, depending upon the dog, its chewing exercise, rate of calcium utilization and many other factors, known and unknown, which affect the development of individual dogs. Diseases, like distemper for example, may sometimes arrest development of the teeth and jaws, which may resume months or even years later.

This is why dogs, especially puppies and young dogs, will often destroy valuable property when their chewing instinct is not diverted from their owners'

his instinct tells him to chew. If your purposes, and those of your dog, are to be accomplished, what you provide for chewing must be desirable from the doggie viewpoint, have the necessary functional qualities, and, above all, be safe.

It is very important that dogs be prohibited from chewing on anything they can break or indigestible things from which they can bite sizeable chunks. Sharp pieces, such as those from a bone which can be broken by a dog, may pierce the intestinal wall and kill.

possessions, particularly during the widely varying critical period for young dogs. Saving your possessions from destruction, assuring proper development of teeth and jaws, providing for "interim" tooth cleaning and gum massage, and channeling doggie tensions into a non-destructive outlet are, therefore, all dependent upon the dog's having something suitable for chewing readily available when

A dog's teeth with little to no calculus build-up, a state achievable through consistent and appropriate care.

Indigestible things which can be bitten off in chunks, such as toys made of rubber compound or cheap plastic, may cause an intestinal stoppage; if not regurgitated, they are certain to bring painful death unless surgery is promptly performed.

NATURAL CHEW BONES

Strong natural bones, such as 4- to 8-inch lengths of round shin bone from mature beef—either the kind you can get from your butcher or one of the varieties available commercially in pet stores—may serve your dog's teething needs, if his mouth is large enough to handle them.

You may be tempted to give your puppy a smaller bone and he may not be able to break it when you do, but puppies grow rapidly and the power of their jaws constantly increases until maturity. This means that a growing dog may break one of the smaller bones at any time, swallow the pieces and die painfully before you realize what is wrong.

Many people have the mistaken notion that their dog's teeth are like those of wild carnivores or of dogs from antiquity. The teeth of wild carnivorous animals and those found in the fossils of the dog-like creatures of antiquity have far thicker and stronger enamel than those of our dogs today.

All hard natural bones are highly abrasive. If your dog is an avid chewer, natural bones may wear away his teeth prematurely; hence, they then should be taken away from your dog when the teething purposes have been served. The badly worn, and usually painful, teeth of many mature dogs can be traced to

excessive chewing on animal bones. Contrary to popular belief, knuckle bones that can be chewed up and swallowed by the dog provide little, if any, useable calcium or other nutrient. They do, however, disturb the digestion of most dogs and might cause them to vomit the nourishing food they really need.

Never give a dog your old shoe to chew on, even if you have removed all the nails or metal parts, such as lace grommets, buckles, metal arches, and so on. Rubber heels are especially dangerous, as the dog can bite off chunks, swallow them, and suffer from intestinal blockage as a result. Additionally, if the rubber should happen to have a nail imbedded in it that you cannot detect, this could pierce or tear the intestinal wall. There is always the possibility, too, that your dog may fail to differentiate between his shoe and yours and chew up a good pair while you're not looking. It is strongly recommended that you refrain from offering old shoes as chew toys, since there are much safer products available.

RAWHIDE CHEWS

The most popular material from which dog chews are made is the hide from cows, horses, and other animals. Most of these chews are made in foreign countries where the quality of the hide is not good enough for

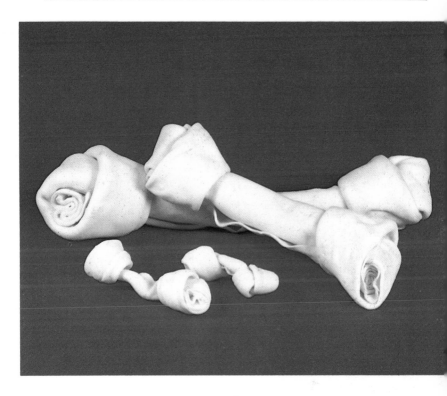

Many dogs love rawhide, and many stores carry a variety of rawhide chew products.

making leather. These foreign hides may contain lead, antibiotics, arsenic, or insecticides which might be detrimental to the health of your dog . . . or even your children. It is not impossible that a small child will start chewing on a piece of rawhide meant for the dog! Rawhide chews do not serve the primary chewing functions very well. They are also a bit messy when wet from mouthing, and most dogs chew them up rather rapidly. They have been considered safe for dogs until recently.

Rawhide is flavorful to dogs. They like it. Currently, some veterinarians have been attributing cases of acute constipation to large pieces of incompletely digested rawhide in ·the intestine. Basically it is good for them to chew on, but dogs think rawhide is food. They do not play with it nor do they use it as a pacifier to relieve doggie tension. They eat it as they would any other food. This is dangerous, for the hide is very difficult for dogs to digest and swallow, and many dogs choke on large particles of rawhide that become stuck in their throats. *Before you offer your dog rawhide chews, consult your veterinarian.* Vets have a lot of

Annealed nylon chews are recommended by veterinarians as proven-safe and effective canine chew devices.

experience with canine chewing devices; ask them what they recommend.

NYLON CHEW DEVICES

The nylon bones, especially those with natural meat and bone flavor added, are probably the most complete, safe, and economical answer to the chewing need. Dogs cannot break them nor bite off sizeable chunks; hence, they are completely safe. And being longer lasting than other things offered for the purpose, they are very economical.

Hard chewing raises little bristle-like projections on the surface of the nylon bones to provide effective interim tooth cleaning and vigorous gum massage, much in the same way your toothbrush does it for you. The little projections are raked off and swallowed in the form of thin shavings, but the chemistry of the nylon is such that they break down in the stomach fluids and pass through without effect.

The toughness of the nylon provides the strong chewing resistance needed for important jaw exercise and effective help for the teething functions; however, there is no tooth wear because nylon is non-abrasive. Being inert, nylon does not support the growth of microorganisms, and it can be washed in soap and water or sterilized by boiling or in an autoclave.

There are a great variety of Nylabone® products available that veterinarians recommend as safe and healthy for your dog or puppy to chew on. These Nylabone® Pooch Pacifiers® usually don't splinter, chip, or break off in large chunks; instead, they are frizzled by the

One of the many advantages of annealed nylon chew products is durability and long life. To keep your Nylabone® products sterile and to re-energize their flavor, these bones can be boiled in broth.

dog's chewing action, and this creates a toothbrush-like surface that cleanses the teeth and massages the gums. At the same time, these hard-nylon therapeutic devices channel doggie tension and chewing frustation into constructive rather than destructive behavior. The original nylon bone (Nylabone®) is not a toy and dogs use it only when in need of pacification. Keeping a bone in each of your dog's recreation rooms is the best method of providing the requisite pacification. Unfortunately, many nylon chew products have been copied. These inferior quality copies are sold in supermarkets and other chain stores. The really good products are sold only through veterinarians, pet shops, grooming salons and places where the sales people really know something about dogs. The good products have the flavor impregnated *into* the bone. This makes the taste last longer. The smell is undetectable

Preventive Dental Care

to humans. The artificial bones which have a strong odor are poor-quality bones with the odor sprayed on to impress the dog owner (not the dog)! These heavily scented dog toys may impart the odor to your carpets or furniture if an odor-sprayed bone lies there wet from a dog's chewing on it.

Food particles can be deposited between the teeth, where they are difficult to remove. Even the best chew products may not be able to free these decaying food pieces. For this reason, the Nylafloss® dental device is recommended. It is the only effective product to clean between the dog's teeth.

While satisfying the deep-rooted desire to chew, the dog's chewing a Gumabone® works to prevent tartar and plaque build-up. A dog should have access to an effective chew product at all times.

FLOSS OR LOSS!

Most dentists relay that brushing daily is just not enough. In order to prevent unnecessary tooth loss, flossing is essential. For dogs, human dental floss is not the answer—however, canine dental devices are available. The Nylafloss® is a revolutionary product that is designed to save dogs teeth and keep them healthy. Even though your dogs won't believe you, Nylafloss® is not a toy but rather

145

Prevention is the key to good dental health. It makes little sense to ignore your dog's dental needs; tooth problems can be costly and detrimental to your dog's well being. Nylafloss® is one very important part of preventive dental care.

a most effective agent in removing destructive plaque between the teeth and *beneath* the gum line where gum disease begins. Gentle tugging is all that is necessary to activate the Nylafloss®. These 100% inert nylon products are guaranteed to outlast rawhide chews by ten times and are available for sale at all pet shops.

THE IMPORTANCE OF PREVENTION

In order to get to the root of canine dentistry problems, it is important for owners to realize that no less than 75% of all canine dental health problems serious enough to require a vet's assistance and nearly 98% of all canine teeth lost are attributable to periodontal disease. Periodontal disease not only mars the teeth but also the gums and other buccal tissue in the mouth. Severe cases of periodontal disease involve resultant bacterial toxins which are absorbed into the blood stream and cause permanent damage to the heart and kidneys. In the infected mouth, teeth are loosened; tartar, unsightly and bad smelling, accumulates heavily; and the dog experiences a complete loss of appetite. Long-standing periodontitis can also manifest itself in simple symptoms such as diarrhea and vomiting.

Periodontal disease deserves the attention of every dog owner—a dog's teeth are extremely important to his ongoing health. The accumulation of plaque, food matter mixed with saliva attaching itself to the tooth surface, is a sure sign of potential bacteria build-up. As toxic material gathers, the bone surrounding the teeth erodes. If plaque and calculus continue to reside without attention, bacteria-fighting cells will form residual pus at the root of the teeth, dividing the gum from the tooth. The debris is toxic and actually kills the buccal tissue. This is a most undesirable situation, as hardened dental calculus is one of the most direct causative agents of periodontitis.

In actuality, the disease is a result of a number of contributing factors. Old age, a diet comprised solely of soft or semi-soft foods, dental tartar, constant chewing of hair and even coprophagy (the eating of stool) are among the most common contributors.

Just as regular dental visits and brushing are necessary for humans, regular hygienic care and veterinary check-ups can help control tooth problems in canines. Involved and expensive routines can be performed on the affected, neglected mouth and teeth if decay has begun

eroding the enamel and infecting the gums. Cleaning, polishing, and scaling are routine to remove calculus build-up.

Owners must claim responsibility for their dog's health, and tooth care is no small aspect of the care required. Daily brushing with a salt/baking soda solution is the best answer, but many owners find this tedious or just too difficult to perform. The simpler and more proven effective way to avoid, reduce, and fight periodontal disease and calculus build-up is giving the dog regular access to a thermoplastic polymer chew device. The Gumabone® products are the only scientifically proven line that offers the desired protection from calculus and tartar build-up.

CANINE DENTAL BREAKTHROUGH

The independent research of Dr. Andrew Duke, D.V.M., reveals that 70% of the dogs that regularly use Gumabone® experience a reduction of calculus build-up. This find is a breakthrough for the dog world, since the Gumabone® has already resided in the toy boxes of many dogs as their favorite play item. Little did owners know previously that their dogs were gaining entertainment and unparalleled dental treatment at the same time. Dr. Duke writes: "There is little debate left that

THE CALCULUS INDEX

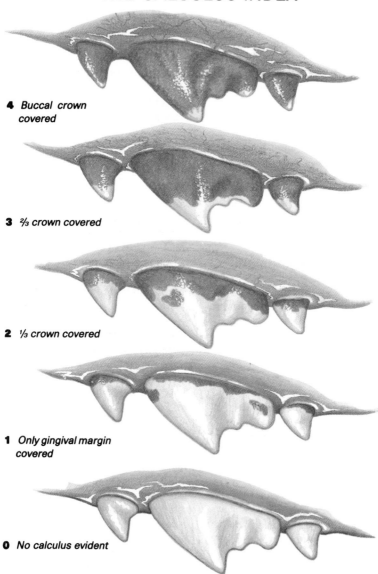

4 *Buccal crown covered*

3 *⅔ crown covered*

2 *⅓ crown covered*

1 *Only gingival margin covered*

0 *No calculus evident*

*An artist's representation of the calculus index, ranging from index rating **4** (topmost drawing) through index rating **0** (lowest drawing).*

dental calculus is an excellent indicator of periodontal health in the dog, just as it is in humans. "Calculus does not cause gingivitis and periodontitis, but the plaque and bacteria that cause periodontitis are responsible for the mineral precipitation we know as 'calculus.' All veterinarians who have made a study of dogs' oral

A dog's teeth showing a moderate calculus build-up.

health have noticed the middle aged dog who actively chews with excellent gingival health. Many of these dogs that chew hard substances regularly wear the cusps down and even may expose the pulp cavity faster than secondary dentin can be formed. Often these 'excellent chewers' are presented with slab fractures of the premolars

or apical abcesses.

"The challenge then becomes to find a substance which is effective in removing calculus and plaque but does not wear the enamel excessively. In an attempt to duplicate the chewstuffs enjoyed by dogs in the wild, researchers have used bovine tracheas to demonstrate the inhibition of plaque and gingivitis. Very little else has been done in veterinary medicine to establish a scientific basis for evaluating chewstuffs.

"In the human field it is generally accepted (incorrectly) that fibrous foodstuffs and diet have no effect on oral health. This is a moot point since the practice of brushing is by far a more efficient technique of preventing plaque accumulation, calculus and periodontal disease. Studies in human subjects failed to find any benefits in eating apples, raw carrots, etc. If people are not allowed to brush, it is difficult to conduct clinical trials of more than one week.

"The increased awareness of animals' dental health of recent years has resulted in most veterinary practitioners' recommending some kind of chewstuff to their dog owners. To meet this market demand, there has been a stampede into the market by vendors ready to promote their products. The veterinarian is furnished no

Plaque is formed by the food debris and bacterial deposits on the teeth. Due to the high carbon dioxide and pH level in the mouth, minerals precipitate on the plaque to form calculus.

scientific data, but is asked to promote rawhide, bounce, and squeaky toys. How would our human colleagues handle this situation? Can Listerine® say that it prevents colds, but not support the claim? Can Tartar Control Crest® or Colgate Tartar Control Formula® be sold if it is not proven that it does in fact reduce tartar? Of course not.

"To this end, the following study was made.

"*Method:* Twenty dogs of different breeds and age were selected from a veterinary practice's clientele. Although most were from multiple pet households, none were colony dogs. The owners were asked if they would allow their dogs to be anesthetized for two prophylactic cleanings which included root planing, polishing, and gingival debridement necessary to insure good oral hygiene.

"The dogs were divided into two groups of 10. Their teeth were cleaned and their calculus index converted to 0. One group was allowed only their normal dry commercial dog ration for 30 days. The other was allowed to have free choice access to Gumabone® products of the appropriate size.

"After 30 days, photoslides were made of the upper 3rd premolar, upper 4th premolar, and the lower 4th premolar on both sides of the dog's mouth. The dogs were again subjected to a prophylactic cleaning and the group reversed. After the second 30 days, photoslides were again made. A total of six teeth in each mouth were evaluated on each dog. This was 80 slides representing 240 teeth."

Fourteen out of 20 dogs (or 70%) experienced a reduction in calculus build-up by regularly

Regular use of the Gumabone® chew products can significantly reduce plaque build-up.

using the Gumabone® product. These products are available in a variety of sizes (for different size dogs) and designed in interesting shapes: bones, balls, knots and rings (and even a tug toy). The entertainment value of the Gumabone® products is but an added advantage to the fighting of tooth decay and periodontitis. The products are ham-flavored and made of a thermoplastic polymer that is designed to outlast by ten times any other rawhide, rubber or vinyl chew product, none of which can promise the proven benefit of the Gumabone®.

If your dog is able to chew apart a Gumabone®, it is probable that you provided him with a bone that is too small for him. Replace it with a larger one and the problem should not re-

Teeth of affected canine showing little to no plaque or calculus build-up after professional cleaning.

Above: *The clean healthy teeth that are desired in dogs should inspire owners to work towards better dental hygiene.* **Below:** *The beginning of undesirable deposits forming on improperly maintained teeth.*

materialize. Economically, the Gumabone® is a smart choice, even without comparing it to the cost of extensive dental care.

Of course, nothing can *substitute* for periodic professional attention to your dog's teeth and gums, no more than your toothbrush can replace your dentist. Have your dog's teeth cleaned by your veterinarian at least once a year—twice a year is better—and he will be healthier, happier, and a far more pleasant companion.

Gumabones® are available through veterinarians and pet shops.

Breeding

If you own a bitch and you want to breed her, first make sure you can handle the responsibility of caring for her and her litter of pups. Consider the time and money involved just to get her into breeding condition and then to sustain her throughout pregnancy and afterwards while she tends her young. You will be obligated to house, feed, groom, and housebreak the puppies until good homes can be found for them; and, lest we forget, there will be periodic trips to the vet for check-ups, wormings, and inoculations. Common sense should tell you that it is indeed cruel to bring unwanted or unplanned puppies into an already crowded canine world; only negligent pet owners allow this to happen. With pet-quality purebred dogs, most breeders require prospective pet owners to sign a neuter/spay agreement when they purchase their dogs. In this way breeders can be assured that only their very best stock of show-quality and breeder-quality animals, i.e., those that match closely their individual standards of perfection and those that are free of genetic disorders or disease, will be used to propagate the breed.

Before you select a stud to mate with your bitch, think carefully about why you want her to give birth to a litter of puppies. If you feel she will be deprived in some way if she is not bred, if you think your children will learn from the experience, if you have the mistaken notion that you will make money from this great undertaking, think again. A dog can lead a perfectly happy, healthy, normal life without having been mated; in fact, spaying a female and neutering a male helps them become better pets, as they are not so anxious to search for a mate in an effort to relieve their sexual tensions. As for giving the children a lesson in sex education, this is hardly a valid reason for breeding your dog. And on an economic level, it takes not only years of hard work (researching pedigrees and bloodlines, studying genetics, among other things), but it takes plenty of capital (money, equipment, facilities) to make a decent profit from dog breeding. Why most dedicated breeders are lucky just to break even. If you have only a casual interest in dog breeding, it is best to leave this pastime to those who are more experienced in such matters, those who consider it a serious hobby or vocation. If you have bought a breeder– or show-quality canine, one that may be capable of producing champions, and if you are just starting out with this breeding venture, seek advice from the seller of your dog, from other veteran breeders, and from your vet before you begin.

Breeding

THE FEMALE "IN SEASON"

A bitch may come into season (also known as "heat" or estrus) once or several times a year, depending on the particular breed and the individual dog. Her first seasonal period, that is to say, the time when she is capable of being fertilized by a male dog, may occur as early as six months with some breeds. If you own a female and your portion of the female's reproductive tract; the soft, flabby vulva indicates her readiness to mate. Around this second week or so ovulation occurs, and this is the crucial period for her to be bred, if this is what you have in mind for her. It is during this middle phase of the heat cycle when conception can take place. Just remember that there is great variation from

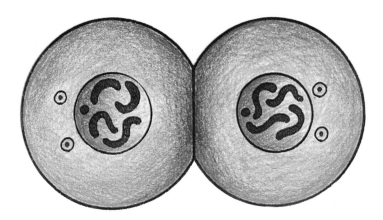

intention is *not* to breed her, by all means discuss with the vet the possibility of having her spayed: this means before she reaches sexual maturity.

The first sign of the female's being in season is a thin red discharge, which may increase for about a week; it then changes color to a thin yellowish stain, which lasts about another week. Simultaneously, there is a swelling of the vulva, the exterior

Cells reproduce by a process called mitosis, in which the cells divide, forming two identical cells.

bitch to bitch with regard to how often they come into heat, how long the heat cycles last, how long the period of ovulation lasts, and how much time elapses between heat cycles. Generally, after the third week of heat, the vulval swelling decreases and the estrus period

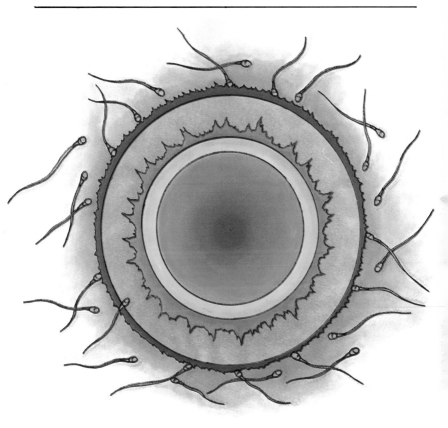

ceases for several months.

It should be mentioned that the female will probably lose her puppy coat, or at least shed part of it, about three months after she has come into season. This is the time when her puppies would have been weaned, had she been mated, and females generally drop coat at this time.

With female dogs, there are few, if any, behavioral changes during estrus. A bitch may dart out of an open door to greet all

The egg within the female is surrounded by a wall that normally takes many sperm to penetrate. In this way, only the strongest sperm will fertilize the egg. A fertile female in season usually has a number of eggs, known as gametes.

available male dogs that show an interest in her, and she may occasionally raise her tail and assume a mating stance, particularly if you pet her lower back; but these signs are not as dramatic as those of the sexually mature male. He himself does not experience heat cycles; rather, he is attracted to the female during all phases of her seasonal period. He usually becomes more aggressive and tends to fight with other males, especially over females in heat. He tends to mark his territory with urine to attract females and at the same time to warn other competitive males. It is not uncommon to see him mount various objects, and people, in an effort to satisfy his mature sexual urges.

If you are a homeowner and you have an absolutely climb-proof and dig-proof run within your yard, it may be safe to leave your bitch in season there. But then again it may not be a wise idea, as there have been cases of males mating with females right through chain-link fencing! Just to be on the safe side, shut her indoors during her heat periods and don't let her outdoors until you are certain the estrus period is over. Never leave a bitch in heat outdoors, unsupervised, even for a minute so that she can defecate or

A whelping box provides the female with a safe place to deliver her pups. Introduce the female to the box several days prior to delivery to get her adjusted to it. Later, when whelping is near, move her to the box so that she may prepare for delivery.

urinate. If you want to prevent the neighborhood dogs from hanging around your doorstep, as they inevitably will do when they discover your female is in season, take her some distance away from the house before you let her do her business. Otherwise, these canine suitors will be attracted to her by the arousing odor of her urine, and they will know instinctively that she isn't far from her scented

While in the womb, each pup is encased within a protective sac.

"calling card." If you need to walk your bitch, take her in the car to a nearby park or field for a chance to stretch her legs. Remember that after about three weeks, and this varies from dog to dog, you can let her outdoors again with no worry that she can have puppies until the next heat period.

Breeding

WHEN TO BREED

It is usually best to breed a bitch when she comes into her second or third season. Plan in advance the time of year which is best for you, taking into account your own schedule of activities (vacations, business trips, social engagements, and so on). Make sure you will be able to set aside plenty of time to assist with whelping of the newborn pups and caring for the dam and her litter for the next few weeks. At the very least, it probably will take an hour or so each day just to feed and clean up after the brood—but undoubtedly you will find it takes much longer if you stop to admire and play with the youngsters periodically! Refrain from selling the litter until it is at least six weeks old, keeping in mind that a litter of pups takes up a fair amount of space by then. It will be your responsibility to provide for them until they have been weaned from their mother, properly socialized, housebroken, and ready to go to new homes (unless you plan to keep them all). Hopefully, as strongly recommended, you will have already lined up buyers for the pups in advance of their arrival into this world.

CHOOSING THE STUD

You can plan to breed your female about six-and-one-half months after the start of her last season, although a variation of a month or two either way is not unusual. Do some research into the various bloodlines within your breed and then choose a stud dog and make arrangements well in advance. If you are breeding for show stock, which will command higher prices than pet-quality animals, a mate should be chosen very carefully. He should complement any deficiencies (bad traits) that your female may have, and he should have a good show record or be the sire of show winners, if he is old enough to have proven himself. If possible, the bitch and stud should have several ancestors in common within the last two or three generations, as such combinations have been known, generally, to "click" best.

The owner of a stud dog usually charges a stud fee for use of the animal's services. This does not always guarantee a litter, but if she fails to conceive, chances are you may be able to breed your female to that stud

Facing page: Dogs have an average gestation period of 63 to 65 days. This chart gives the expected delivery date according to the date on which the bitch was mated. The due date is an approximation only, and the owner should be prepared well in advance of the due date, especially with first-time mothers. If a bitch is mated more than once, the owner should use the date of the first mating but realize the possibility of a later delivery.

PERPETUAL WHELPING CHART

Label	Days
Bred—Jan.	1 2 3 4 5 6 7 8 9 10 11 12 13 14 15 16 17 18 19 20 21 22 23 24 25 26 27 28 29 30 31
Due—March	5 6 7 8 9 10 11 12 13 14 15 16 17 18 19 20 21 22 23 24 25 26 27 28 29 30 31 — April 1 2 3 4
Bred—Feb.	1 2 3 4 5 6 7 8 9 10 11 12 13 14 15 16 17 18 19 20 21 22 23 24 25 26 27 28
Due—April	5 6 7 8 9 10 11 12 13 14 15 16 17 18 19 20 21 22 23 24 25 26 27 28 29 30 — May 1 2
Bred—Mar.	1 2 3 4 5 6 7 8 9 10 11 12 13 14 15 16 17 18 19 20 21 22 23 24 25 26 27 28 29 30 31
Due—May	3 4 5 6 7 8 9 10 11 12 13 14 15 16 17 18 19 20 21 22 23 24 25 26 27 28 29 30 31 — June 1 2
Bred—Apr.	1 2 3 4 5 6 7 8 9 10 11 12 13 14 15 16 17 18 19 20 21 22 23 24 25 26 27 28 29 30
Due—June	3 4 5 6 7 8 9 10 11 12 13 14 15 16 17 18 19 20 21 22 23 24 25 26 27 28 29 30 — July 1 2
Bred—May	1 2 3 4 5 6 7 8 9 10 11 12 13 14 15 16 17 18 19 20 21 22 23 24 25 26 27 28 29 30 31
Due—July	3 4 5 6 7 8 9 10 11 12 13 14 15 16 17 18 19 20 21 22 23 24 25 26 27 28 29 30 31 — August 1 2
Bred—June	1 2 3 4 5 6 7 8 9 10 11 12 13 14 15 16 17 18 19 20 21 22 23 24 25 26 27 28 29 30
Due—August	3 4 5 6 7 8 9 10 11 12 13 14 15 16 17 18 19 20 21 22 23 24 25 26 27 28 29 30 31 — Sept. 1
Bred—July	1 2 3 4 5 6 7 8 9 10 11 12 13 14 15 16 17 18 19 20 21 22 23 24 25 26 27 28 29 30 31
Due—September	2 3 4 5 6 7 8 9 10 11 12 13 14 15 16 17 18 19 20 21 22 23 24 25 26 27 28 29 30 — Oct. 1 2
Bred—Aug.	1 2 3 4 5 6 7 8 9 10 11 12 13 14 15 16 17 18 19 20 21 22 23 24 25 26 27 28 29 30 31
Due—October	3 4 5 6 7 8 9 10 11 12 13 14 15 16 17 18 19 20 21 22 23 24 25 26 27 28 29 30 31 — Nov. 1 2
Bred—Sept.	1 2 3 4 5 6 7 8 9 10 11 12 13 14 15 16 17 18 19 20 21 22 23 24 25 26 27 28 29 30
Due—November	3 4 5 6 7 8 9 10 11 12 13 14 15 16 17 18 19 20 21 22 23 24 25 26 27 28 29 30 — Dec. 1 2
Bred—Oct.	1 2 3 4 5 6 7 8 9 10 11 12 13 14 15 16 17 18 19 20 21 22 23 24 25 26 27 28 29 30 31
Due—December	3 4 5 6 7 8 9 10 11 12 13 14 15 16 17 18 19 20 21 22 23 24 25 26 27 28 29 30 31 — Jan. 1 2
Bred—Nov.	1 2 3 4 5 6 7 8 9 10 11 12 13 14 15 16 17 18 19 20 21 22 23 24 25 26 27 28 29 30
Due—January	3 4 5 6 7 8 9 10 11 12 13 14 15 16 17 18 19 20 21 22 23 24 25 26 27 28 29 30 31 — Feb. 1
Bred—Dec.	1 2 3 4 5 6 7 8 9 10 11 12 13 14 15 16 17 18 19 20 21 22 23 24 25 26 27 28 29 30 31
Due—February	2 3 4 5 6 7 8 9 10 11 12 13 14 15 16 17 18 19 20 21 22 23 24 25 26 27 28 — March 1 2 3 4

again. In some instances the owner of the stud will agree to take a "first pick of the litter" in place of a fee. You should, of course, settle all details beforehand, including the possibility of a single puppy surviving, deciding the age at which the pup is to be taken, and so forth.

If you plan to raise a litter that will be sold exclusively as pets,

and if you merely plan to make use of an available male (not a top stud dog), the most important selection point involves temperament. Make sure the dog is friendly, as well as healthy, because a bad disposition can be passed on to his puppies—and this is the worst of all traits in a dog destined to be a pet. If you are breeding pet-quality dogs, a "stud fee puppy," not necessarily the choice of the litter, is the usual payment. Don't

The reproductive system of the female dog consists of a highly specialized group of organs situated at the rear of the animal.

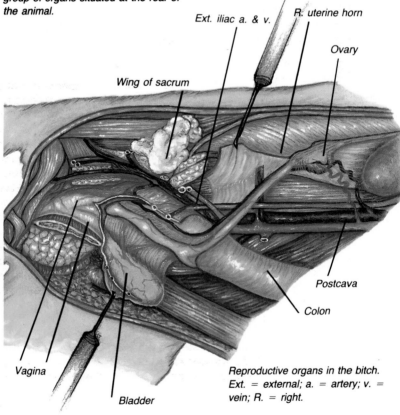

Reproductive organs in the bitch. Ext. = external; a. = artery; v. = vein; R. = right.

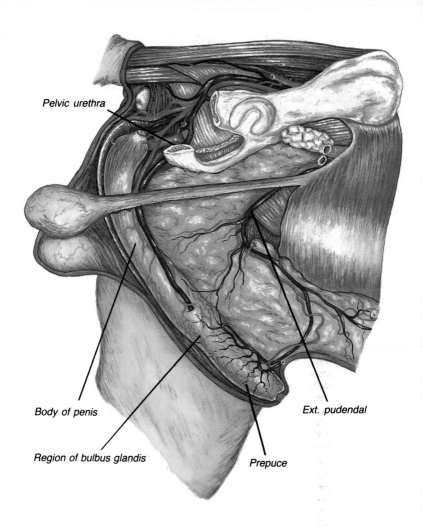

Pelvic urethra

Body of penis

Region of bulbus glandis

Ext. pudendal

Prepuce

The reproductive system of the male dog includes the penis and testicles. The sperm and testosterone producing testes are contained within the scrotal sac. When not excited, the penis is withdrawn into the dog. The dog's penis is unique in that the base of the shaft has a bulbous swelling that forbids retraction from the vagina until some time has passed after intercourse.

breed indiscriminately; be sure you will be able to find good homes for each of the pups, or be sure you have the facilities to keep them yourself, *before* you plan to mate your dog.

PREPARATION FOR BREEDING

Before you breed your female, make sure she is in good health.

She should be neither too thin nor too fat. Any skin disease *must* be cured first so that it is not passed on to the puppies. If she has worms, she should be wormed before being bred or within three weeks after the mating. It is generally considered a good idea to revaccinate her against distemper and hepatitis before the puppies are born. This will increase the immunity the puppies receive during their early, most vulnerable period.

The female will probably be ready to breed twelve days after the first colored discharge appears. You can usually make arrangements to board her with the owner of the stud for a few days, to insure her being there at the proper time; or you can take her to be mated and bring her home the same day if you live near enough to the stud's owner. If the bitch still appears receptive she may be bred again two days later, just to make certain the mating was successful. However, some females never show signs of willingness, so it helps to have an experienced breeder on hand. In fact, you both may have to assist with the

The canine uterus is quite different from the human uterus. Besides the difference in shape, the canine uterus is designed to house an average of five to eight offspring.

OVARY

HORN OF UTERUS

BLADDER →

BODY OF UTERUS

CANINE UTERUS
Before mating

VAGINA

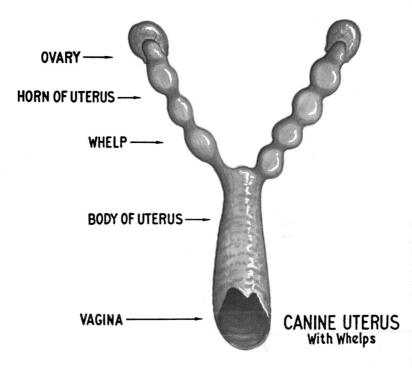

OVARY →

HORN OF UTERUS →

WHELP →

BODY OF UTERUS →

VAGINA ⟶

CANINE UTERUS
With Whelps

Prior to birth, the developing pups are housed in the horns of the uterus.

mating by holding the animals against each other to ensure the "tie" is not broken, that is, to make certain copulation takes place. Sometimes, too, you'll need to muzzle the bitch to keep her from biting you or the stud.

Usually the second day after the discharge changes color is the proper time to mate the bitch, and she may be bred for about three days following this time. For an additional week or so, she may have some discharge and attract other dogs by her odor; but she should not be bred. Once she has been bred, keep her far from all other male dogs, as they have the capacity to impregnate her again and sire some of her puppies. This could prove disastrous where purebred puppies—especially show-quality ones—are concerned.

THE FEMALE IN WHELP

You can expect the puppies nine weeks from the day of the mating, although sixty-one days is as common as sixty-three. Gestation, that period when the pups are developing inside their mother, varies among individual bitches. During this time the female should receive normal care and exercise. If she was overweight at the start, don't increase her food right away; excess weight at whelping time can be a problem with some dogs. If she is on the thin side, however, supplement her meal or meals with a portion of milk and biscuit at noontime. This will help build her up and put weight on her.

You may want to add a mineral and vitamin supplement to her diet, on the advice of your veterinarian, since she will need an extra supply not only for herself but for the puppies growing inside of her. As the mother's appetite increases, feed her more. During the last two weeks of pregnancy, the pups grow enormously and the mother will have little room for food and less of an appetite. She should be tempted with meat, liver, and milk, however.

As the female in whelp grows heavier, cut out violent exercise

Using simple genetic rules, an owner can predict to some degree the traits that the offspring of a given mating can exhibit. The six possible ways in which a pair of determiners can unite are illustrated on this Mendelian expectation chart. Ratios apply to expectancy over large numbers, except in lines 1, 2, and 6 where exact expectancy is realized in every litter.

MENDELIAN EXPECTATION CHART

and jumping from her usual routine. Although a dog used to such activities will often play with the children or run around voluntarily, restrain her for her own sake.

A sign that whelping is imminent is the loss of hair around her breasts. This is nature's way of "clearing a path" so that the puppies will be able to find their source of nourishment. As parturition draws near, the breasts will have swelled with milk and the nipples will have enlarged and darkened to a rosy pink. If the hair in the breast region does not shed for some reason, you can easily cut it short with a pair of scissors or comb it out so that it does not mat and become a hindrance to the suckling pups later on.

PREPARING FOR THE PUPPIES

Prepare a whelping box a few days before the puppies are due, and allow the mother to sleep there overnight or to spend some time in it during the day to become accustomed to it. This way she is less likely to try to have her pups under the front porch or in the middle of your bed. A variety of places will serve, such as the corner of your cellar or garage (provided these places are warm and dry). An unused room, such as a dimly lit spare bedroom, can also serve as the place for delivery. If the weather is warm, a large outdoor dog house will do, as long as it is well protected from rain, drafts, and the cold—and enclosed by fencing or a run. A whelping box serves to separate mother and puppies from visitors and other distractions. The walls should be high enough to restrain the puppies yet low enough to allow the mother to take a short respite from her brood after she has fed them. Four feet square is minimum size (for most dogs) and six-to-eight-inch high walls will keep the pups in until they begin to climb; then side walls should be built up so that the young ones cannot wander away from their nest. As the puppies grow, they really need more room anyway, so double the space with a very low partition down the middle of the box, and soon you will find them naturally housebreaking themselves. Puppies rarely relieve themselves where they sleep. Layers of newspapers spread over the whole area will make excellent bedding and be absorbent enough to keep the surface warm and dry. These should be removed daily and replaced with another thick layer. An old quilt or washable blanket makes better footing for the nursing puppies than slippery newspaper during the first week; this is also softer for the mother to lie on.

Be prepared for the actual whelping several days in

advance. Usually the mother will tear up papers, refuse food, and become restless. These may be false alarms; the real test is her temperature, which will drop to below 100°F (38°C) about twelve hours before whelping. Take her temperature with a rectal thermometer, morning and evening, and usher her to her whelping box when her temperature goes down. Keep a close watch on her and make sure she stays safely indoors (or outdoors in a safe enclosure); if she is let outside, unleashed, or allowed to roam freely, she could wander off and start to go into labor. It is possible that she could whelp anywhere, and this could be unfortunate if she needs your assistance.

WHELPING

Usually little help is needed from you, but it is wise to stay close to be sure that the mother's lack of experience (if this is her first time) does not cause an unnecessary complication. Be ready to help when the first puppy arrives, for it could smother if she does not break the amniotic membrane enclosing it. She should tear open the sac and start licking the puppy, drying and stimulating it. Check to see that all fluids have been cleared from the pup's nostrils and mouth after the mother has licked her youngster clean; otherwise the pup may

have difficulty breathing. If the mother fails to tear open the sac and stimulate the newborn's breathing, you can do this yourself by tearing the sack with your hands and then gently rubbing the infant with a soft, rough towel. The afterbirth attached to the puppy by the long umbilical cord should follow the birth of each puppy. Watch to be sure that each afterbirth is expelled, for the retention of this material can cause infection. In her instinct for cleanliness the mother will probably eat the afterbirth after severing the umbilical cord. One or two meals of this will not hurt her; they stimulate her milk supply, as well as labor, for remaining pups. However, eating too many afterbirths can make her lose appetite for the food she needs to feed her pups and regain her strength. So remove the rest of them, along with the wet newspapers, and keep the box dry and clean.

If the mother does not bite the cord or bites it too close to the puppy's body, take over the job to prevent an umbilical hernia. Tearing is recommended, but you can cut the cord, about two inches from the body, with a sawing motion with scissors that have been sterilized in alcohol. Then dip the end of the cut cord in a shallow dish of iodine; the cord will dry up and fall off in a few days.

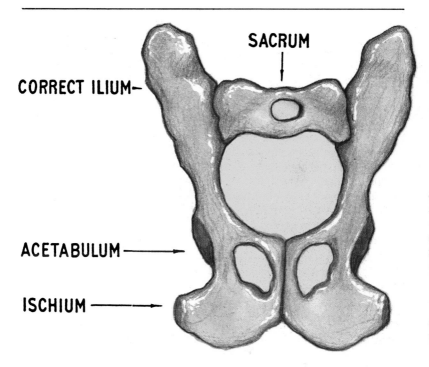

Shape of pelvic entrance in the average female dog, showing adequate aperture through which the whelps have to pass.

The puppies should follow each other at intervals of not more than half an hour. If more time goes past and you are sure there are still pups to come, taking the mother for a brisk walk outside may start labor again. If she is actively straining without producing a puppy, the youngster may be presented backward, a so-called "breech" birth. Careful assistance with a well-lubricated finger to feel for the puppy or to ease it back may help, but never attempt to pull it out by force. This could cause serious damage, so seek the services of an expert—your veterinarian or an experienced breeder.

Even the best planned breeding can bear unexpected problems and complications. Therefore, do not rely solely on textbook knowledge of breeding and genetics. Experienced breeders and veterinarians will generally lend their words of wisdom—take full advantage of their generosity. Mere trial and error is no basis for any responsible breeding program.

If *anything* seems wrong during labor or parturition, waste no time in calling your veterinarian, who will examine the bitch and, if necessary, give her hormones to stimulate the birth of the remaining puppies. You may want his experience in whelping the litter even if all goes well. He will probably prefer to have the puppies born at his hospital rather than getting up in the middle of the night to come

A puppy nurser kit is considered standard equipment by many breeders. These kits are available at your local pet shop.

to your home. The mother would, no doubt, prefer to stay at home; but you can be sure she will get the best of care in a veterinary hospital. If the puppies are born at home, and all goes as it should, watch the mother carefully afterward. Within a day or two of the birth, it is wise to have the veterinarian check her and the pups to ensure that all is well.

Be sure each puppy finds a teat and starts nursing right away, as these first few meals supply colostral antibodies to help him fight disease. As soon as he is dry, hold each puppy to a nipple for a good meal without competition. Then he may join his littermates in the whelping box, out of his mother's way while she continues giving birth. Keep a supply of puppy formula on hand for emergency feedings or later weaning. An alternative formula of evaporated milk, corn syrup, and a little water with egg yolk can be warmed and fed if necessary. A pet nurser kit is also a good thing to have on hand; these are available at local pet shops. A supplementary feeding often helps weak pups (those that may have difficulty nursing) over the hump. Keep track of birth weights and weekly readings thereafter; this will furnish an accurate record of the pups' growth and health, and the information will be valuable to your veterinarian.

RAISING THE PUPPIES

After all the puppies have been born, take the mother outside for a walk and drink of water, and then return her to take care of her brood. She will probably not want to stay away for more than a minute or two for the first few weeks. Be sure to keep water available at all times and feed her milk or broth frequently, as she needs nourishment to produce milk. Encourage her to eat, with her favorite foods, until she seeks them of her own accord. She will soon develop a ravenous appetite and should have at least two large meals a day, with dry food available in addition. Your veterinarian can guide you on the finer points of nutrition as they apply to nursing dams.

Prepare a warm place to put the puppies after they are born to keep them dry and to help them to a good start in life. An electric heating pad, heat lamp or hot water bottle covered with flannel can be placed in the bottom of a cardboard box and near the mother so that she can see her puppies. She will usually allow you to help her care for the youngsters, but don't take them out of her sight. Let her handle things if your interference seems to make her nervous.

Be sure that all the puppies are getting enough to eat. If the mother sits or stands instead of lying still to nurse, the probable cause is scratching from the puppies' nails. You can remedy this by clipping them, as you would the bitch's, with a pet nail clipper. Manicure scissors also do for these tiny claws. Some breeders advise disposing of the smaller or weaker pups in a large litter, as the mother has trouble handling more than six or seven. You can help her out by preparing an extra puppy box or basket furnished with a heating pad and/or heating lamp and some bedding material. Leave half the litter with the mother and the other half in the extra box, changing off at two-hour intervals at first. Later you may exchange them less frequently, leaving them all together except during the day. Try supplementary feedings, too. As soon as their eyes open, at about two weeks, they will lap from a small dish.

WEANING THE PUPPIES

Normally the puppies should be completely weaned at five weeks, although you can start to feed them at three weeks. They will find it easier to lap semi-solid food than to drink milk at first, so mix baby cereal with whole or evaporated milk, warmed to body temperature, and offer it to the puppies in a saucer. Until they learn to lap it, it is best to feed one or two at a time because they are more likely to walk into it than to eat it. Hold the saucer at their chin level, and let them gather around, keeping paws off

Breeding

Excessively long puppy nails can scratch the whelping mother's tummy and teats, making the bitch little inclined to nurse the pups. Specially designed clippers for trimming the nails are available at your local pet shop.

the dish. Cleaning with a damp sponge afterward prevents most of the cereal from sticking to the pups if the mother doesn't clean them up. Once they have gotten the idea, broth or babies' meat soup may be alternated with milk, and you can start them on finely chopped meat. At about four weeks, they will eat four meals a day and soon do without their mother entirely. Start them on canned dog food, or leave dry puppy food with them in a dish for self-feeding. Don't leave the water dish with them all the time; at this age everything is a play toy and they will use it as a wading pool. They can drink all they need if it is offered several times a day, after meals. As the puppies grow up, the mother will go into their "pen" only to nurse them, first sitting up and then standing. To dry up her milk

supply completely, keep the mother away for longer periods; after a few days of part-time nursing she can stay away for even longer periods, and then permanently. The little milk left will be resorbed by her body.

The puppies may be put outside during the day, unless it is too cold or rainy, as soon as their eyes are open. They will benefit from the sunlight. A rubber mat or newspapers underneath will protect them from cold or dampness. As they mature, the pups can be let out for longer intervals, although you must provide them with a shelter at night or in bad weather. By now, cleaning up after the matured youngsters is a man-sized job, so put them out at least during the day and make your task easier. If you enclose them in a run or kennel, remember to clean it *daily*, as various parasites and other infectious organisms may be lurking if the quarters are kept dirty.

You can expect the pups to need at least one worming before they are ready to go to new homes. Before the pups are three weeks old, take a stool sample from each to your veterinarian. The vet can determine, by analyzing the stool, if any of the pups have worms—and if so, what kind of worms are present. If one puppy is infected, then all should be wormed as a preventive measure. Follow the veterinarian's advice; this also applies to vaccinations. You will want to vaccinate the pups at the earliest possible age. This way, the pups destined for new homes will be protected against some of the more debilitating canine diseases.

THE DECISION TO SPAY OR NEUTER

If you decide not to use your male or female for breeding, or if you are obligated to have the animal altered based on an agreement made between you and the seller, make the necessary arrangements with your veterinarian as soon as possible. The surgery involved for both males and females is relatively simple and painless: males will be castrated and females will have their ovaries and uterus removed. In both cases, the operation does not alter their personalities; you will, however, notice that males will be less likely to roam, to get into fights with other male dogs, and to mount objects and people.

Your veterinarian can best determine at what age neutering or spaying should be done. With a young female dog, the operation may be somewhat more involved, and as a result be more costly; however, in the long run you will be glad you made the decision to have this done for your pet. After a night or two at the veterinarian's or an animal hospital, your bitch can be safely returned to your home. Her stitches will heal in a short time, and when they are removed, you will hardly notice her souvenir scar of the routine operation. Once she has been spayed, she no longer will be capable of having a litter of puppies. Pet adoption agencies and other animal welfare organizations can house only so many animals at one time, given the money, space, and other resources they have available. This is why pet owners are urged to have their pets altered, so that puppies resulting from accidental breedings won't end up being put to sleep as so many others have that are lost, stray, unwanted, or abandoned.

Top view of a dog's skeletal structure. The dog is a highly specialized animal.

Dogs and the Law

By Anmarie Barrie, Esq.

This chapter is written merely as a general survey of the laws pertaining to dogs. The laws vary tremendously from jurisdiction to jurisdiction. They also change over time, and are subject to the interpretation of the controlling authorities.

Any reference to a resource material or facility is not an endorsement.

As civilization advances and living conditions become more crowded, laws are created to keep society functioning smoothly. Our lives become more regulated. This includes how we care for our dogs.

Laws dealing with dogs are in effect at all levels of government. Mostly, though, dog law is a local affair. There are many dog laws. They vary from country to country and from city to city. However, there are general rules and guidelines that are common to all dog laws.

BUYING AND SELLING

Most of the law regulating buyers, sellers, and breeders of dogs pertains to dealers. A dealer is a person who buys and sells dogs in the regular course of his business. Therefore, an owner who sells the family pet's puppies at a yard sale is not covered. However, some laws do encompass the occasional seller.

If you regularly sell, keep, or breed more than a certain number of dogs, you may need a kennel or breeder's license. Puppies may or may not be included in this number. Usually diseased dogs, and dogs under a specified age, are forbidden to be sold.

Whether you are the buyer or the seller, put the sales agreement in writing. Until you write it out, you may not realize that you and the other party have different understandings. The agreement should include, but is certainly not limited to, the following:

1. Breed, sex, age, color, quality, and birth date of the dog
2. Names and addresses of

the buyer and the seller

3. Name and address of the breeder

4. Names and registration numbers of the sire and dam (pedigree)

5. Date of the last veterinary exam, the name and address of the veterinarian, and any findings

6. Date and types of vaccinations

7. Behavior (viciousness) and propensities (training) of the dog

8. Any health problems the dog may have

9. Any warranties (guarantees) the seller is making

10. The name of the original owner (if the seller purchased the dog from someone else).

GENERAL GUIDELINES FOR DOG OWNERS

Licenses

Probably wherever you live, a dog needs a license. A license involves a fee and usually has to be renewed periodically. It should be worn by the dog at all times. Puppies under a certain age are exempt from the licensing requirements. A license may cost less for a spayed or neutered dog, an assistance dog, or a dog belonging to an old or disabled person. To find out where to get a license, talk to your pet shop owner, veterinarian, local officials, the animal control or health department, or look in the telephone book.

Licensed and unlicensed dogs may be accorded different treatment under the law. Any unlicensed dog, or a dog running at large without a license tag, may be impounded. Unlicensed dogs that are impounded are destroyed or sold sooner than licensed dogs, because local authorities are unable to trace ownership. Furthermore, some authorities permit the killing of an unlicensed dog, or a licensed dog not wearing its license, at any given time. Yet a dog wearing a license can be killed only if it is attacking a person or livestock.

Dogs and the Law

If your dog is lost or stolen, it will be harder to find if it does not have a license. An owner of an unlicensed dog may be subject to a fine or penalty.

Vaccinations

A current rabies vaccination is a common requirement. Other inoculations, such as a distemper shot, may be necessary as well. Proof of vaccination may be required in order to get a license. Puppies under a certain age are not required to be vaccinated.

Leash Laws

Many areas have leash laws. These laws require a dog to be under the control of its owner at all times. This may involve confinement, that the dog be on a leash, or even muzzled.

No dog should be allowed to roam free. A dog at large could be impounded and disposed of according to regulations. Its owner may be fined and have to pay for the cost of confining the dog. Some communities have special areas where dogs are allowed to run loose.

Other Restrictions

Muzzle laws are becoming more popular, as are laws requiring owners to clean up their dog's solid waste (pooper-scooper laws) if deposited anywhere off their own property. Many buildings, such as restaurants, apartments, and hotels, and other areas, such as beaches, are strictly off limits to dogs. Owners of assistance dogs are commonly excluded from these laws.

You should also be aware that some municipalities actually prohibit a dog from being left alone in a car. An owner may be violating anti-cruelty laws.

How Many Dogs Allowed?

Many animal lovers have more than one dog. However, some communities restrict the number of dogs allowed per household, and some residencies refuse to permit dogs at all.

These laws are taken quite seriously. If your condominium or apartment lease has a no-pets clause, you can be evicted for harboring a dog. If your residence limits the number of dogs you can keep, exceeding that number can subject you to a daily fine.

If you want to keep more dogs, you may need to apply for a city permit or a kennel license. This may entail extra fees, rules, and inspections.

An owner may be required to dispose of the number of dogs exceeding the allowable limit. Fines and jail sentences can be imposed as well. These enforcement measures can be imposed even if you are caring for someone else's dog only temporarily. Puppies less than a certain age may or may not be exempted.

Lost and Found

If your dog is lost, call any agency you think handles dogs. Include the police, health and animal control departments, and humane societies. Listen to local radio stations and read the local newspapers that list found animals. Visit the police station,

animal shelter, and government offices where lists may be posted. Leave a picture and an accurate description of the dog every place you visit. If at first you are not successful, keep asking around. The dog may show up later.

If you find a dog, attempt to find its owner, or give the dog to the local authorities. If you do not make an effort to return the dog to its owner, you may be liable to the owner for the value of the dog. The law may require you to notify the animal control authorities.

If the dog remains in your possession, check for

identification. The dog may have the name and address of its owner on a tag. Call the owner. If the dog has a license tag, call the agency that issued the tag to get the name of the owner.

Ask local residents if they recognize the dog. Post signs around the area where the dog was found. Put a notice in the paper and notify the local radio station.

Impoundment laws often give animal control officials the authority to pick up, impound, sell, and/or destroy dogs. However, since a dog is considered the personal property of its owner, a dog cannot be confiscated without notice, and possibly a hearing.

An owner's property rights may be lost, though, under certain conditions. Any unlicensed dog, or a dog running at large without a vaccination tag, or running at large without a license tag may be impounded without first notifying its owner.

Dogs running around loose are

typical pound inhabitants. Injured, abandoned, and vicious dogs also end up at the pound. A dog that has bitten a person, caused damage, or been declared a nuisance can be taken from its owner and impounded. An owner who has his dog in his possession, though, is entitled to be notified before the dog is seized. An owner must usually be notified again before the dog is destroyed.

A pound is required to keep the dog for a prescribed period of time before it can take action. If the owner can be identified, he must be notified. To reclaim the dog, an owner may have to have the dog licensed, vaccinated, pay a fine, and pay a charge for every day that the dog is kept. If the owner does not claim the dog, it can be sold, offered for adoption, or killed in a humane manner. The law may allow a dog to be given to an assistance dog agency or a research facility.

Dog laws may be enforced by any number of agencies. These include the police, a humane society, an animal control center, or a health department. No matter which organization is responsible for enforcing the law, all of them must respect the legal rights of an owner.

Burial

Contact your local animal control authority for information on how to dispose of your dog's remains. You may not be permitted to bury the dog on your own property. You may have to bring the dog's body to a pet cemetery. The wisest thing to do is to have your vet handle the burial. Some towns will dispose of the dog for a fee.

DOGS AS PROPERTY

A dog is personal property. This fact has a lot of legal implications, because an owner of property has legally enforceable rights. The law prohibits a person from injuring, taking, or destroying the property of another. So an owner who has a property interest in his dog is entitled to compensation if his dog is killed, stolen, or injured.

Damages typically include actual out-of-pocket expenses. But other criteria may have some bearing as well. For example, consider the market value and age of the dog. Its type, traits, pedigree, and purchase price are all legitimate concerns. The feelings of the owner will probably not be considered in a damage award. Other considerations include registration, breeding value,

value as a watchdog, and if the dog is expecting a litter.

For an owner to enforce his rights as an owner of property, the dog may need to be licensed. An owner of an unlicensed dog may not be afforded any protection under the law. An owner of a puppy that does not yet require a license should still benefit from the property laws concerning dogs.

Since a dog is not a person, it cannot be a beneficiary of a will. It cannot inherit money or other property. If you want your dog to be cared for after your death, you must designate a new owner for the dog in your will. It is wise to leave money to the new owner to care for your dog. Be sure to consider medical expenses—as your dog gets older, its veterinary bills will increase.

A dog may be contested property in a divorce proceeding. A court will determine custody and visitation rights.

Property cannot be taken from an owner without due process of the law. This means that the dog owner must have notice, and possibly be given a hearing before his property is taken or destroyed. Therefore, before a dog can be impounded, killed, or offered for adoption, its owner must be given adequate notice. The amount of time considered "adequate notice" varies from place to place and may depend on whether or not the dog is licensed.

Who is Responsible for the Dog?

An owner is legally responsible for controlling his dog. However, the definition of an owner may be broad enough to include the legal owner, as well as anyone who cares for, harbors, or has custody of the dog. So someone besides the owner, or more than one person, may be liable for the actions of the dog.

A dog owner may be a minor. In such a situation, the youngster's parents or legal guardian may be responsible for any injury or damage caused by the dog. Under certain circumstances, a landlord may be responsible. The landlord must have known that a tenant's dog was dangerous, have had

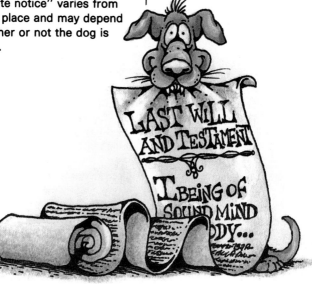

Dogs and the Law

the power to remove the dog, but did nothing about it.

A veterinarian and his staff members may be injured by a dog during the course of its treatment. The dog owner is probably not responsible because these people know and accept the risk of injury. Of course, an owner cannot conceal the fact that his dog is dangerous. A doctor has insurance to cover these mishaps.

Liability for Damage and Injury

Typically, an owner is legally liable for any personal injury or property damage (including killing livestock) caused by his pet. Depending upon the circumstances, an owner may be fined or jailed as well.

An owner may have to pay medical expenses. This can include costs for doctors, hospitals, medications, physical therapy, and counselling. A victim may also be entitled to compensation for loss of earnings if he was out of work due to his injury. The time off may involve both treatment and recuperation.

Some victims of dog attacks are awarded compensation for pain and suffering. The amount of the award can vary tremendously depending on the circumstances because it is difficult to calculate the cost specifically. Sometimes a spouse or close relative can receive compensation as well. The theory is loss of service of the injured person. Loss of service is not limited to economics; it may also include loss of companionship.

If the fault on the part of the owner is particularly shocking or reckless, an award may be doubled or even tripled. Additionally, the victim may be entitled to punitive damages. This recovery punishes the owner's poor conduct by making him pay even more than the amount considered adequate compensation to the victim. The financial status of the owner can be taken into account when establishing a punitive damage award.

Also, the owner will have to take measures designed to prevent further detriment. In serious cases, this could mean destruction of the dog. Since any dog can cause injury or damage under the right circumstances, a prudent owner will take precautionary measures designed to prevent his dog from causing harm.

There are several legal theories under which dog owners may be found liable for their dog's acts. Some of the

theories are strict liability, common law rules, negligence, and nuisance. Strict liability means that the owner is responsible for the dog's actions even though the owner is not at fault in any way. Common law doctrines are defined in court decisions. They are not codified in statutes. An owner is negligent if he does not exercise reasonable and ordinary care in controlling his dog. A dog is a nuisance if it unreasonably and substantially offends or inconveniences a person.

Often there is an on-duty exemption for trained police or military dogs. The police or government may be immune from liability if the injury occurred because the dog was provoked or while it was working.

Vicious Dogs

Once a dog has bitten or exhibited menacing behavior, it may be officially declared a vicious dog. Dogs that have been trained to attack or fight may also be considered vicious. A few dog breeds are believed to be inherently dangerous.

Owners of such vicious dogs may be required to take further measures to control their dogs. The dogs may have to be securely confined at all times, on a leash and muzzled when in public, and have a special vicious dog license. The dog may have to be tattooed. The owner may be required to have liability insurance for the dog. Signs may be necessary to warn the public that a vicious dog is in residence. A bond may have to be posted with the municipality to cover any potential injury or damage. Some cities ban vicious dogs.

An owner who fails to comply with the law may be fined or jailed. He may also be liable for double or triple the amount of damage caused by the dog. The dog may be impounded and killed.

Preventing Injury

If you are a dog owner or keeper, the best way to avoid liability is to prevent injury. Adhere to a few common sense rules to keep risk of harm to a minimum.

No matter how small, old or timid the dog is, it can hurt someone, damage property, or be a nuisance. Any dog may bite or scratch if it is threatened, or if it is protecting its owner, its puppies, or its food. A dog racing around a corner or barking unexpectedly may startle an unsuspecting person and result in injury.

Therefore, keep your dog securely contained in the house or yard. Be sure it cannot escape to scare or otherwise get in the way of strangers. Post warning signs that alert passers-by that a dog is present. Never let your dog off its leash to run at large. The owner must be in control at all times.

Lastly, keep the dog's license and vaccinations up-to-date. If your dog does manage to get free, its return will be more expedient if it is properly identified. The less time out of your care, the less time the dog has to cause trouble. Should the dog bite someone, the dog will not need to be quarantined if its rabies vaccine is current.

183

Dogs and the Law

Insurance

The cost of the potential damage and injury inflicted by a dog can be enormous. A wise owner will check to see that his homeowner's or renter's policy covers his dog. A dog that has a menacing behavior should have its own insurance coverage. Dangerous and vicious dogs may be obligated by law to have liability insurance.

A typical homeowner's or renter's insurance plan covers any damage caused by the policy holder's negligence. This coverage often extends to incidents that take place away from the owner's property, even if a vehicle is involved. If policy does not extend to vehicular events, look to your auto insurance plan. Some insurance companies refuse to issue a policy altogether if a vicious dog lives in the home.

Often a plan limits its coverage to the first instance of harm caused by a dog. After that, the owner must pay out of his own pocket. Other companies exclude certain types of dog-related harm from their coverage. This is why it is important to read your policy carefully. If you do not understand the terms, call your agent for an explanation. It is important to know your liability before an accident occurs.

If your home and auto insurance do not extend to dog-related injuries, or you think the coverage is not broad enough, buy insurance for your pet. Take out insurance that will protect you and the dog while at home and/or away.

Your dog may become ill or injured. Get coverage that will pay for its medical expenses. Some insurance firms offer pet health insurance. These policies may pay for medications, doctors' bills, and hospital fees.

Handling a Controversy

A dog can be dangerous, or it can be just a nuisance. Either way, if you have a dog like this in your neighborhood, or if it is your dog, you may be involved in a dispute. Your dog may have caused injury or damage, or your dog may have been the victim. Either way, you should be prepared to handle the controversy in a responsible and legally acceptable manner.

A dog may not be dangerous, but it can be a nuisance. Some irksome antics include digging up a yard, chasing a car, scattering garbage across the lawn, ravaging a prized garden, barking incessantly, roaming the neighborhood, and frightening people.

If you are the property owner, the first thing to do is to talk to the owner of the dog. Use a reasonable and friendly approach—*avoid animosity*. Offer your neighbor some advice as to how to stop the dog's bad habits. Suggest obedience school or calling the local humane society for some tips. If the dog's poor behavior stops, call on your neighbor again to thank him for taking the necessary measures.

If you happen to be the owner of the dog wreaking havoc, be understanding, not hostile. After all, you are responsible for keeping your dog from annoying your neighbors. Your neighbor has probably had several encounters with your dog before he came to talk to you. Take the proper measures to stop the

dog's poor behavior. After a few days, visit your neighbor to be sure the problem has been solved.

If talking to your neighbor is a dead-end, try mediation. This method of settling disputes outside of a courtroom involves the imposition of a neutral third party. This individual acts as a link between the disputing parties to keep the lines of communication open. A mediator does not choose sides, he merely identifies problems and suggests compromises. Once the differences are settled, define the terms in a writing

Dogs and the Law

signed by both parties.

There may be a reason that you do not want to talk to your neighbor, or talking to him proves disastrous, or maybe you just do not know who owns the troublesome dog. Call your police, animal control department, health or public safety authorities. The people responsible for controlling dogs can call or visit the dog owner, or even issue a citation.

Look up all the pertinent local law, such as ordinances dealing with noise, vicious dogs, leash laws, nuisances, dogs running at large, personal injury, property damage, or the number of dogs allowed per household, and have it enforced. Enlist the aid of other neighbors who are annoyed. And, most importantly, be persistent.

You may be compelled to go to court. If so, familiarize yourself with the law so that you can make sure your complaint meets all the required elements. Good preparation is vital to presenting a sound argument. Be brief and articulate, not boring. Present your case in an organized manner. You may be allowed to present witnesses, and to utilize documents, police reports, hospital records, medical bills, and photographs. Avoid confusion or repetition. But most importantly, always be respectful to both the judge and your adversary.

CRUELTY

In most modern societies, cruelty against dogs is forbidden. Inhumane treatment may include intentional abuse, neglect, theft, abandonment, and dog fighting. Cropping ears and tails without using anesthesia, leaving a dog which was hit by your car, confining a dog in a parked car, and poor conditions in a shelter may all be considered cruelty. In Great Britain, ear cropping is expressly prohibited. It is lawful, though, to kill a dog in the act of injuring a person or damaging property. Using dogs for scientific research is usually not punishable by law, even though it is distasteful.

If you suspect improper behavior, first talk to the owner. If the maltreatment does not cease, report the abuse to the humane society, the police, a local dog society, or anyone else you think has the right to take action. It is best to have the complaint in writing. Keep a copy for yourself.

Except in the case of an emergency, the dog owner is entitled to notice before his dog can be taken away. A mistreated dog is seized by the authorities and impounded. If the cruelty is particularly outrageous, the abuser may be subject to a fine or a jail sentence.

TRAVEL

It is a common sight to see a

dog owner traveling with his pet. In fact, many owners refuse to go anywhere without their dog. However, most owners do not realize that traveling is stressful for their pet. So if you are not going to leave your dog at home, at least make the trip as comfortable as possible.

Restrictions regarding pet travel are constantly changing due to health and international situations. Therefore, call the appropriate agricultural department, embassy, or consulate before departing. Most countries require a recent certificate of health. Vaccinations may be necessary.

Of course, your dog should be properly identified. A tag with the dog's name, and your name, address, and phone number should be attached to the dog at all times.

Each container should be plainly marked, labeled, or tagged on the outside with the names and addresses of the shipper and the consignee. An accurate invoice statement specifying the number of each species contained in the shipment must also be included.

Since the hours of service and the availability of inspectors vary from port to port, check with your anticipated port of arrival prior to importation. This will reduce the possibility of unnecessary delay.

An airline may refuse to transport an animal unless specific criteria are met. Common restrictions include that the dog must be at least eight weeks old; certified as healthy; secured in a carrier; and adequately identified.

A dog traveling on an airline must be contained in a shipping crate. The crate should be sturdy and well ventilated. It should be large enough to allow your pet to stand, turn around, and lie down comfortably. The carrier should be marked "Live Animals" and "This End Up." Your name, address, and phone number, the dog's name, and the destination should be on the crate.

LANDLORDS AND DOGS

Many landlords prefer not to rent to dog owners. A dog can disturb other tenants if it is noisy, messy, or smelly. Under the right circumstances, any dog can destroy property or injure a person. A landlord can experience a lot of aggravation and expense. Violation of an existing no-pets clause may be a sufficient cause for eviction or a penalty.

A no-dogs policy may be negotiable. An exception may be made if the prospective tenant can assure the landlord that the dog will not be a problem. But how do you convince the landlord?

There are several things that can be done. Introduce the dog to the landlord. The landlord can see for himself that the dog is well groomed and well mannered. An untrained puppy is not as desirable as a mature, adult dog. A spayed or neutered dog will probably get bonus points. Bring along written references from previous landlords and neighbors saying that the dog has not been a problem and is well liked.

Special provisions can be negotiated in private leases that are fair to both sides. Dog owners are still responsible for damage and injury caused by their dogs.

Index

Lost dogs, 175–177
Lyme Disease, 132
Medicine, administration, 123; liquid and pill, 123
Mendelian expectation chart, 164
Mice, 131
Micro filaria, 1365
Mitosis, 154
Mosquito bites, 136
Muzzle, emergency, 122–123, 126; laws, 174
Neighbors, 185
Neutering, 153
Newspapers, used for punishment, 89
New York Academy of Dog Training, 95
Nightshade, 127
Nurser, puppy, 168
Nursing dams, feeding and, 168
Nylabone®, as chew product, 51; as exercise tool, 118; as pacifier, 71, 117; as therapeutic device, 142, 143; as toy, 111; nylon balls, 85
Nylafloss®, for dental hygiene, 145, 146
Nylon chews, 142–143
Nylon discs, 81
Nylon toys, 114–118
Obedience trial equipment, 97
Old dogs, 136–137; vitamins and, 137
Ovaries, removed, 170
Overfeeding, 67
Ovulation, 154
Pack instincts, 105
Pads, foot, injury to, 113
Paper training, 88, 89
Parainfluenza, 132
Parasites, control of, 77; external, 133; internal, 135
Parvovirus, 131–132
Pedigree papers, 46, 47, 48

Pelvic entrance, 167
Penis, 161
Periodontal disease, 146–147
Perpetual whelping chart, 159
Planned departures, 110–111
Plaque, 147
Poisoning, 118–119; 120–121
Pokeweed, 55
Polyurethane toys, 82, 118
Pooch Pacifiers®, 117, 143
Pooper-scooper laws, 174
Pregnancy, and appetite, 164; and exercise, 164; and hair loss, 165
Punishment, 95, 102–103; delayed, 89
Rabies, 129–131
Rats, 130
Rawhide, 140–142, 149
Registration papers, 46, 48
Restraining a dog, 128
Restrictions regarding dogs, 189
Road accidents, 124
Roundworms, 135
Routine, in feeding, 65; in training, 51
Running away, 95
Sacrum, 167
Selection, adult or pup, 43–44; male or female, 42–43
Self-feeding, 62
Selling litters, 158
Sexual urges, male's, 156
Shock, signs of, 124
Show-quality, 153
Socialization, 91
Spaying, 42, 153, 154
"Speak," barking and, 101, 102
Stable fly, 132
Stifle joint, 79

Stud dog, 158–159
Supplements, food, 62; vitamin and mineral, 63, 164
Surrogate mothers, 58
Symptoms of illness, 113
Tapeworm, 133, 135; cycle of, 137
Tartar, 138
Temperature, as sign of labor, 165; bodily, 113
Territory, male's, 156
Ticks, 132, 133
Tooth care, professional, 152
Toys, 80; hard rubber, 114; nylon, 114–118
Training, 91–101; "Come", 98; "Down", 99–100; "Heel", 98; "Sit", 96; "Stay", 96–97
Training collars, 93
Travel, 122; restrictions regarding dogs, 188
Tug toys, 84
Umbilical cord, 166
Umbilical hernia, 166
United Kennel Club, 47
Uterus, before mating, 162; with whelps, 163
Vaccination, 162; for pups, 170; laws regarding, 173
Veterinary care, 112
Veterinary check-ups, 51
Vicious dogs, laws regarding, 181
Vitamins, older dogs and, 137
Vomiting, induced, 119
Water bucket approach, 103
Water hemlock, 120
Weaning, 169–170
Whelping, 158, 166–168; bitch and, 163–165; box, 156, 165; chart, 159
Whipworms, 135
Wills and dog, 189
Worming, for pups, 170
Yew, 55

Required Reading

The Atlas of Dog Breeds of the World By Bonnie Wilcox, DVM, & Chris Walkowicz (H-1091)
Traces the history and highlights the characteristics, appearance and function of every recognized dog breed in the world. 409 different breeds receive full-color treatment and individual study. Hundreds of breeds in addition to those recognized by the American Kennel Club and the Kennel Club of Great Britain are included—the dogs of the world complete! The ultimate reference work, comprehensive coverage, intelligent and delightful discussions. The perfect gift book. *Hard cover, 9" × 12", 912 pages, 1,106 color photos. ISBN 0-86622-930-2*

Dog Training By Lew Burke (H-962)
The elements of dog training are easy to grasp and apply. The author uses the psychological makeup of dogs to his advantage by making them want to be what they should be—substituting the family for the pack. *Hard cover, 5½" × 8", 255 pages, 64 black and white photos, 23 color photos. ISBN 0-87666-656-X*

The Complete Dog Buyer's Guide By Dr. William Bruette & Kerry V. Donnelly (H-989)
Plots the advances in veterinary care and genetics of the last fifty years by incorporating descriptions of the breeds as they are today. Many of the photos illustrate Best In Show winners and top and historical dogs. Individual complete sections on breeding, selection, caring, etc. *Hard cover, 5½" × 8", 608 pages. Illustrated. ISBN 0-86622-026-7*

The Mini Atlas of Dog Breeds By Andrew De Prisco & James B. Johnson (H-1106)
An identification handbook giving a concise and thorough look at over 400 of the world's dog breeds. The authors' enthusiastic and knowledgeable approach brings to life instantly man's oldest friend and companion. A flowing and witty text, further enlivened by 500 full-color photos, successfully maps out the world of dogs; an easy-reference format pinpoints each breed's development, portrait, registry, and pet attributes. The volume is captioned with specially designed symbols. *Hard cover, 5½" × 8½", 544 pages, nearly 700 color photos. ISBN 0-86622-091-7*

Dog Owner's Encyclopedia of Veterinary Medicine By Allan H. Hart, B.V.Sc. (H-934)
Written by a vet who feels that most dog owners should recognize the symptoms and understand the cures of most diseases of dogs so they can properly communicate with their veterinarian. This book is a necessity for every dog owner, especially those who have more than one dog. *Hard cover, 5½" × 8", 186 pages, 86 black and white photos. ISBN 0-87666-287-4*

Dog Breeding for Professionals By Dr. Herbert Richards (H-969)
For dog owners who need and actively seek good advice about how to go about breeding their dogs whether for profit or purely because of their attachment to animals. *Please note* that the breeding photography is sexually explicit and some readers may find it offensive. *Hard cover, 5½" × 8", 224 pages, 105 black and white photos, 62 color photos. ISBN 0-87666-659-4*

Dogs and the Law By Anmarie Barrie, Esq. (DS-130)
A practical and reliable survey of laws pertaining to our dogs. Advice concerning liability, licenses, impoundment, vehicles, insurance, wills, vaccinations and many other useful and often entertaining topics. Full color cartoon illustrations add a delightful twist. *Hard cover, 6" × 9", 160 pages, over 55 color illustrations, appendices, charts. ISBN 0-86622-088-7*